RUSKIN COLLEGE

RUSKIN COLLEGE

Contesting knowledge, dissenting politics

Edited by
Geoff Andrews, Hilda Kean and
Jane Thompson

Lawrence & Wishart
LONDON

Lawrence & Wishart Limited
99a Wallis Road
London E9 5LN

First published 1999

British Library Cataloguing in Publication data.
A catalogue record for this book is available from the
British Library.

ISBN 0 85315 899 1

Typeset by
Derek Doyle & Associates, Liverpool.
Printed and bound in Great Britain by
Redwood Books, Trowbridge.

Contents

INTRODUCTION

Geoff Andrews, Hilda Kean, Jane Thompson

That Ruskin College reached its centenary must have surprised many. The founders perhaps would despair that such institutions are still needed. Former students of the 1960s and 1970s might wonder why the place has not been torn apart by internal dissent. Staff who left the College in the 1980s and 1990s might wonder at the tenacity of current students and staff, and their determination for the place to succeed against the tide of neo-liberalism and technical rationality that has swept through education in recent years. Few who know the place would regard its centenary as an uncontentious event: even the organisation for the celebrations in February 1999 provoked strong disagreements: views ranged from scrapping the event completely to emulating an Oxford college gaudy.

Controversy, derived as much from Ruskin's relationship to the external political and educational world as from the disparate views of its staff and students, has been a constant in the college's history. Established in 1899, a year before the founding of the Labour party, Ruskin was intended to provide residential education for working-class men (women were first admitted as residential students in 1919) to enable them to enter into public political life. Unsurprisingly, the debates which characterised early Labour conferences re-surfaced within Ruskin. The difficulty facing the college was whether students were to be encouraged to support their own working-class communities and agitate for political change, or whether they had to be developed as exceptional individuals who were capable of discarding their class-based allegiances. This issue preoccupied the student strikers at Ruskin in 1909 who wanted a curriculum embodying class consciousness, and also the college authorities who advocated the latter stance and managed successfully to rebut the students' challenge. The 1908 report, *Oxford and working class education*, drawn up jointly by Ruskin College, Oxford University and the Workers' Educational Association, aligned the college more closely with the university. Students for decades to come worked towards an Oxford University diploma, yet the underlying tensions about the labour movement remained. Speakers at the college are as likely to be Labour prime ministers – Callaghan first launched his attacks on progressive education in schools at Ruskin in 1976 and Blair his blueprint for standards in the run up to the 1997 election – as those critical of labourism. Arthur Scargill, Tony Benn, sacked Liverpool dockers or Hillingdon hospital cleaners are amongst the dissenting campaigners given a platform at Ruskin in the 1990s.

This book is not a contribution to the genre of commemorative histories. We do not believe such a book could, or should, be usefully written about Ruskin, especially at this time. Commemoration by its very nature implies agreement on what is to be celebrated and a desire to see a moment in the past, or an institution, frozen sufficiently in time to create a particular memory. Many of the chapters in this book do discuss the importance of the past in understanding why Ruskin has been the site of struggle and dissent. And historical practice has always been strong within the College. But, as Paul Martin discusses, this has frequently been within frameworks outside conventional practices. The past historical legacy of Ruskin, particularly of Raphael Samuel, is significant, but is explored here in order to situate current historical practice inside and outside the College. There may be continuity in pedagogic practices – democratic scholarship, 'history from below' – but the focus of inquiry, of knowledge, has changed and has contemporary relevance.

Although we do not intend to evoke or create particular memories, we do want to explore the way in which Ruskin students and staff have acted at particular significant moments, and the nature of such moments. These are not focused solely on the College, in the sense of there being a particular Ruskin time separate from the maelstrom of life. Rather the events to which we refer in the past life of the College – the founding ideals, the strike of 1909, the first British women's liberation movement conference in 1970, Northern Ireland civil rights action by former students, or support for the miners in the 1980s – take their impetus from politics outside the College. It has been the willingness to engage with politics of the real world which has both characterised the distinctive nature of Ruskin and, inevitably, ensured that there is no internal agreement over knowledge or politics. Significantly, as several contributors indicate, there never was a heyday of Ruskin when there was an homogeneity of outlook on matters educational or political.

As Nick Kneale indicates, even the first years of the College were characterised by sharp debates on the nature of 'the Ruskin ideal' – a construction of a particular form of working-class masculinity fiercely debated in the pages of *Young Oxford*. Roger Fieldhouse addresses some of the specific debates around the role and curriculum of Ruskin in relation to the labour movement, Oxford University, the WEA and the Labour College movement in the early years of the College. Other contributions draw out the impact of later events on the nature of politics and contested knowledge within the curriculum. As Geoff Andrews argues, the debate in the 1980s over the future of the left in the wake of the miners' and printers' defeat did not meet with any sort of consensus within the College: indeed the positions of David Selbourne and Raphael Samuel both epitomised and helped to create the debates of the wider labour movement. Even radical events of the 1960s and 1970s, which students organised with great enthusiasm, lacked a unified political perspective, as Bob Purdie suggests in his chapter.

The practice of Ruskin is not fixed. Like the world outside – and inside – it changes. Even the building itself epitomises political contestation, with changing iconography reflecting, for example, the contribution of women to the life of the College; and the rehabilitation of the former disgraced principal Dennis Hird is reflected in the reinstallation of his portrait, as Hilda Kean discusses in her chapter.

Jane Thompson suggests that the purpose and focus of the College is still more idiosyncratic than coherent, and that it has lost its dialectical and organic relationship with progressive social movements. To survive and flourish in the future Ruskin must rejuvenate its philosophic base in radical politics and democratic education. But as the left has been sharply divided over strategies, so too has there been dissent within Ruskin about its future direction – and the way in which its past legacy might be seen. Ruskin itself embodies the contradictions implicit in government policy, a contradiction stressed by Richard Bryant in his survey of student poverty. How can there be challenging lifelong learning for mature students on the margins when there is insufficient funding for students to be able to live and engage in learning and personal and social change?

When Ruskin reached its century there was some publicity: a celebratory programme on Radio 4, and articles in the local press and *Times Higher Education Supplement*. But it didn't gain national press coverage in 1999 until there was a suggestion that, because recruiting students was a problem, the College was in crisis. As many other institutions in further and higher education find, recruiting working-class students is a real issue when most of them do not have the financial ability to commit themselves to study – even for a year. Students face extremely reduced circumstances with no hope of a job at the end, and burgeoning debt through loans for university studies. While the commemoration of Ruskin's existence did not invite much media interest, its possible absence did. This was not a story of a small college 'with local difficulties' but of a national institution, called erroneously by an *Observer* article 'working class Eton'. That it should merit a feature in the Sunday press perhaps says something about the way the College is seen as out of time but apparently 'known' to its readership. That the images the article presented of 'success' stories were entirely of white male trade unionists and Labour MPs says much about the way in which its public persona is rooted in an homogenised idea of the past, removed from its present constituencies.

Single mothers surviving poverty and successfully juggling home, childcare and study, Afro-Caribbean students who are not drug dealers, or white working-class men in their 50s studying for the sheer heck of it are not the subject matter of sexy media fascination. That Ruskin College remains committed to both equality of access and excellence in academic standards, bucking the national trend, suggests it still has a distinctive place in progressive British society. That students choose to study courses which challenge preconceptions – green economics, feminist action (even in these 'post feminist' days), discrimination and the law, radical, socialist and feminist political movements and community action, for example – suggests that there is still a place for dissent and for continuing discussion about what people really want to know. And this has nothing to do with being at Eton.

We do not outline here what direction Ruskin should take in the future: those debates will take place in other contexts. If this collection raises questions, creates knowledge and provokes debate (and anger) it will have served a purpose – of engaging anew with ideas and of continuing a tradition firmly established within Ruskin of contesting knowledge within a framework of political activity and dissent.

The editors want to thank David Horsfield and Bill Dewhurst for their help with sources and processes.

'The science and art of man-making': Class and gender foundations of Ruskin Hall, Oxford, 1899

NICK KNEALE

To Walter Vrooman, one of the founding fathers of Ruskin Hall writing in the 1899 first edition of the College magazine *Young Oxford*, education was essentially 'the Science and Art of man-making'.[1] This telling phrase points towards several key sites of class and gender conflict that underpinned the foundations of a college which to many observers had at best 'an unrealistic future'.[2] As we shall see, this process of a cultural reshaping of the working man gave rise to fascinating tensions between the manly and the effeminate, the labourer and the scholar, the practical and the aesthetic, the revolutionary and the evolutionary, the modern and the ancient. Struggling for economic and ideological survival in a city alien to many, dwarfed by a university which had always seemed 'an hotel and club for gentlemen', the students and educators of Ruskin Hall laboured energetically to establish a permanent identity.[3] Inevitably, there were some heavy casualties in this fight to reclaim knowledge and social standing from a strongly empowered bourgeoisie, not least among the ranks of those women who were denied equal access to an education which remained centred patriarchally on the working man. Moreover, the ethic of manliness adopted by the College was in some ways a crude throwback to mid-Victorian ideals of moral earnestness and physical health at a time when new emotional possibilities for men had been carved out painfully by such Oxford figures as Oscar

Wilde. But for all the failings in the early years of the Ruskin Hall Movement, a spirit of defiance and progress remained. 'Remember', we are told consistently with pride and intent to bring about lasting social change, 'the workman has a culture of his own that the scholar possesses not'.[4]

The Ruskin Hall Movement quickly gained a colossal momentum after the opening of the College in February 1899. By the end of the first two years, in addition to the resident body, eighteen hundred correspondence students were enrolled and local Ruskin Halls had been set up in Manchester, Liverpool, Birmingham and Stockport.[5] Yet the symbolic centre of the Movement was always Oxford. By the time the Hall was renamed Ruskin College and moved to its present site in Walton Street in 1903, the provincial Halls had begun to close as other provisions for mass education came into force. The birth of a new, working-class college in Oxford had its own specific cultural connotations. While ceremonially laying a foundation stone for the Walton Street building in 1912, Sydney Buxton reportedly quipped that for early students of the Hall, who had seen the splendour of the University buildings, 'it must have been somewhat of a disillusionment when they were pointed to Ruskin College'.[6] Somewhat sycophantically, Buxton went on to express 'a real debt of obligation' to 'the University itself for the assistance which was given in various ways to Ruskin College' in its early years from 1899. The cultural critic should always be wary of attempts by the enfranchised classes to assimilate and control a potentially anarchic and dispossessed underclass. Brian Simon has pointed out that, after the Labour victories of 1906, 'there was a concerted effort by the University "towards subsuming the college under the University"'.[7] Seeking to allay the fears of University interference which had inflamed the infamous 1909 Ruskin student strike, Sidney Ball, a Fellow of St John's, explained at the 1912 ceremony how this 'spirit of intellectual patronage was not offered in a spirit of patronage, still less with any desire to impregnate the students with middle-class economics, but in a spirit of friendship and fellowship'.[8] As we shall see, such a rhetoric, which consciously seeks to deny the bourgeois desire to 'impregnate' the working classes with knowledge, while fostering an ethos of male bonding and 'fellowship', was to have important class and gender implications in the first few years of Ruskin Hall.

From the outset, the founders were keen to emphasise the College's total autonomy from the University. Thus it was widely reported that 'Ruskin Hall has no connection with the University of Oxford; it is altogether outside its rules and regulations'.[9] Yet, despite all best efforts, many observers did wrongly interpret the project as a magnificently charitable gesture on the part of the University. The *Manchester Guardian* reported that the 'Alma Mater' of Oxford University had allowed its 'young residents' to 'help poorer Britain to the riches of an educated mind' amongst its 'paradise of gardens'.[10] A correspondent from Italy observed that 'at Oxford the students of the University (the real one) hold meetings to advise ways of encouraging the Ruskin student, and lend their work'.[11] While there was indeed a large amount of goodwill towards Ruskin Hall from individuals associated with the University, such reports obscure the overarching educational differences between the two separate institutions. It would appear that some unfortunate young upper-class dandies did indeed mistake Ruskin Hall for a college of the University. Edmund Stonelake, a Welsh Miner who came to Ruskin in the summer of 1901, recalls the arrival of a 'breezy fellow' who was 'flashily dressed, with loud yellow shoes and red tie. He appeared to be fairly well off financially' and 'spent most of his time on the river'.[12] The relatively harsh regime at the college meant that such students did not tend to stay long. Nor did several lecturers who had attempted to use the College to further their standing in the academic community. As Bertram Wilson commented in a statement to the Executive Committee in 1909, now held in the Ruskin College archives, in the early days, 'all kind of odd lectures were given by any wandering lecturer who came along and who wanted to say that he had lectured in Oxford'. This association of Oxford with a peculiar kind of superiority which was simultaneously academic and social, while undoubtedly conferring certain benefits upon the new college, gave to the birth of Ruskin Hall a puzzling complexity.

There were indeed some famous commentators attracted by this unique set of cultural circumstances. In a letter which outlines his reasons for declining to lecture at the College, George Bernard Shaw argued that 'a workman *ought* to have a vulgar prejudice against Oxford'. Shaw questioned the ideological validity of the entire Ruskin Hall scheme, since the working man 'will learn nothing here that he cannot learn anywhere else, except the social tone, which will be as detrimental to him as a workman as it is useful to a gentleman'. He goes on to express his fear that by such an Oxford education the Ruskin man will be debased 'from a workman into a schoolman'.[13] This is unfortunate, as the Hall undoubtedly needed men of Shaw's intellectual calibre and profile in the early years. Yet it is also perceptive, as there is evidence to suggest that some Ruskin men were indeed seduced away from their class roots by the heady charms of Oxford life. Thus, in *Young Oxford*, we find descriptions by Ruskin students which are reminiscent of the most purple prose by a university freshman and dispel any sense of class discontent: 'The sculls dip into the water, and flash out into the moonlight, causing the boat to become the centre of living radiancy; and anon we hear the church bells chiming softly through the evening stillness. Our trip ends, we are happy, quietly happy'.[14] *The General Circular of Ruskin Hall, Oxford* had stated that 'it is not intended that a man should rise out of his class' but should lead a life 'worthy of a citizen and a man'. As Shaw seemed to sense, how could a falsely contented man, living a life of Oxford leisure, return to the harsh realities of the factory floor?

Those with a vested interest in maintaining the social and educational status quo were equally suspicious of Ruskin Hall, not because it would render the working-class man docile, but would on the contrary whip him up into a frenzy of revolutionary fervour. W.W. Craik has argued that the College was initially treated with 'cold indifference' as 'an undesirable intrusion' by its more illustrious and established neighbour.[15] In March 1899, the Oxford Union held a debate with the motion 'that in the opinion of this House a University of the people is an impossibility', at which it was argued that Ruskin Hall would 'be no more than an educational sausage machine for the turning out of Labour agitators'.[16] On the opening of the College, one commentator alleged that it could 'serve no useful purpose' beyond creating 'spouters or agitators', for 'the simple reason that in proportion as they are taught and fitted for something better' they will 'cease to be work-men'.[17] This anxiety about the fluidity of class boundaries, and the dangers of raising people out of their allotted social position, was a common one at the end of a century which had seen the overthrow of feudal, land-based relationships by the social instability of industrialised life in the city. It was, simply put, becoming more and more difficult to keep the masses down, and out of education. As one Ruskin correspondence student bluntly stated, 'I have a friend who writes me that my study will only tend ... "to give me the hump"'.[18]

Another heavyweight of Victorian thought, the evolutionary theorist, Herbert Spencer, was strikingly candid in his reasons for refusing to lecture at Ruskin Hall. As well as being 'profoundly averse to the teachings of Mr. Ruskin', he blusters, 'I am also averse to socialism in all its manifestations'. Clearly, Spencer did not feel that the advancement of the lower orders was good for the progress of society as a whole. As though for good measure, he adds, 'I also disapprove of free libraries and have declined in any way to help them'.[19] This is richly ironic in that many of the essays written by Ruskin Hall men in *Young Oxford* from 1899 to 1903 show the deepest respect for Spencer's sociological thought. Indeed, he is given the hallowed title of one of a select band of 'Men who have Helped Us', along with other prominent 'manly' figures such as Thomas Carlyle, Alfred Tennyson and John Ruskin himself.[20]

But the linkage between politically aware, dangerously intellec-tualised working-class men and the threat of revolution was a hard one to break. In 1899, *Punch* concocted a satirical interview with Ruskin Hall men:

> 'And are you on strike?'
> 'Generally, in term-time.'
> 'But doesn't that interfere with your work rather?'
> 'Oh, no! We are learning to be Labour leaders'.[21]

There were, to the delight no doubt of the sceptics, clashes between Ruskin students and the supposedly better educated university men. One early Ruskin student, Jack Lawson, recalls how he and his friends 'used the most lurid language about the capitalist class and pointedly included Oxford University'.[22] Ruskin men were in equal measure mocked for their cultural difference by the University undergraduates. As Lawson recounts,

> I remember one of our men, who spoke with a Cockney accent, at one meeting, with a sweep of the arms, included the assembled undergrads as the bourgeoisie. But he called it BOW-JER-WOW-SIE. Every time he said 'Bow-jer-wow-sie' there was a bow-wow-wow like the bark of a pack of dogs from the men in cap and gown. The end of it was a fist fight.

However, these class and educational differences were not as irreconcilable as many pessimists had predicted and, as Lawson points out, 'there was a good deal of personal friendship with the undergrads'.[23] Edmund Stonelake, too, reports that he made 'acquaintance with the student sons of wealthy men, who met me on equal terms with no trace or sign of snobbery'.[24] There was in fact a great deal of effort on behalf of both sides to break out of the destructively stereotypical opposition between Ruskin 'agitators' and university 'snobs'. In the words of one Ruskin commentator, 'by the proper organisation of human life, the rich will be equal gainers with the poor' – so that one day the world will have 'outgrown the necessity for any class antagonism'.[25]

As one correspondence student, a Shropshire agricultural labourer, neatly put it, the Ruskin students came to 'favour evolution rather than revolution'.[26] To bring about what were described as such 'peaceful revolutions', advancement by education and thought rather than by agitation and brute force came to be the Ruskin Hall ideal of social change.[27] Attempts were made to rationalise the reasons behind mass insurrection and the early 'Elementary Psychology' course even contained papers on 'Pathological, Physiological, and Mob Psychology'.[28] Such seemingly reasonable attitudes went someway towards allaying the fears of outside observers. In March 1899, *The Clarion* tried to reassure its readers that Ruskin Hall, under the guidance and 'health' of the Principal, Dennis Hird, would 'make constructors of society, moulders, not frothy revolutionists'.[29] Yet, as the 1909 student strike was to prove, the potential for swift and radical direct action always lay beneath this intellectual veneer of gradual social change. When cherished principles were challenged (and, in the case of the Strike, the authority of the socialist Principal was under threat from a university influenced Board), Ruskin students were revolutionaries at heart.

On the very first page of *Young Oxford* is an illustration which shows a diminutive yet upright Ruskin Hall, embodied as Ruskin the 'road-mender' with pick and shovel in hand, confronting the decayed and monolithic Sphinx of Oxford University.[30]

Plate 1: Oxford University - and Ruskin Hall

Source: *Young Oxford*, Vol.1, No.1, October 1899, p3.

One of those 'Men who have Helped Us', the Scottish man of letters Thomas Carlyle, had famously written of the Sphinx as an alluring yet treacherous woman, fascinating yet ruinous to man.[31] In a clever appropriation of this symbolism, the Ruskin Hall illustrator depicts Oxford University as the embodiment of the deceptive, decayed and effeminised fixity of the educated ruling classes. As an anti-type to this feminine decadence stands Ruskin the road-mender, erect, mobile and manly. At the College's opening ceremony, Charles Vrooman described the naming of Ruskin Hall as a 'feeble attempt to honour the name of a great man'.[32] At his death in 1900, Ruskin was venerated by Ruskin students as being among 'the ranks of England's heroes and saints'.[33] Indeed, there was much in Ruskin's copious writings from which the working man could draw inspiration. P.D. Anthony has summed up Ruskin's key social theory as stating 'that at whatever cost in productivity or profit, the engagement of the workmen's mind in what they do in work must be achieved to prevent their decay and the decay of their society'.[34] Ruskin's social criticism placed the working man at the very core of society.

Yet this adoption of John Ruskin as the champion of the working classes in the face of an Oxford-educated elite is somewhat problematical. By 1899 he was a spent force both as a thinker and as a man. As the biographer Joan Evans points out, insane and near the end of his life, Ruskin 'could take no pleasure ... in the establishing of a College for Working Men at Oxford that bore his name'.[35] Moreover, Ruskin's work on social change was always considered to be inferior to his art criticism. One of the first courses on the Ruskin Hall 'Literature and Art' programme of 1899 was designed 'to acquaint the student with the social, educational *and* art ideals of John Ruskin'.[36] It was indeed difficult not to consider Ruskin's writings on art as his greatest achievement. It is Ruskin as supreme aesthete and not as social commentator, as intellectual labourer rather than radical reformer, which was and has remained the enduring image of the man who had been made the Slade Professor of Fine Art at Oxford University in 1869. There is thus a paradox at the very centre of the figure taken to be the symbol of manliness for the new college. Ruskin the man embodied not only virility and strength, but a feminine and potentially feminising perception of beauty in art.[37] What is more, he was for most of his life a central pillar in the old educational regime, a lauded son of Oxford University.

The somewhat false image of Ruskin the labourer derives from his ill-fated 'road mending' project of 1874, in which teams of Oxford undergraduates were seduced by his fine prose into improving conditions for the agrarian poor at Hincksey.[38] Ruskin had sought to distinguish constructive labour from the idle pursuits of the leisured classes, pronouncing that 'even digging, *rightly* done, is at least as much an art as the mere muscular act of rowing'.[39] His use of the term 'muscular' here is by no means a casual one. From the turn of the nineteenth century, the middle-class ideal of manliness, as exemplified in novels such as Thomas Hughes's *Tom Brown's Schooldays*, had been founded on a rhetoric of moral and physical health.[40] This popular intellectual movement, which linked sane manliness to physical prowess and thus 'defined itself and its agenda through direct references to the male body', came to acquire the label Christian Socialism or, less sympathetically, 'Muscular Christianity'.[41] One of the founding fathers of this movement was F.D. Maurice, who in 1854 had solicited Ruskin's help in the establishing of a Working Men's College in London. Cultural historians are divided as to the motives behind this early drive to educate the labouring poor. While Derek Leon describes the scheme as a harmonious joining of radical intellectuals and the disenfranchised masses, Patrick Brantlinger argues more convincingly that it was an attempt to control the destructive forces of a potentially revolutionary underclass.[42] Ruskin himself was sceptical of the benefits of any bookish education which was irrelevant to the necessities of modern life – 'you do not educate a man by telling him what he knew not, but by making him what he was not'.[43]

Ruskin's ideals of social equality were indeed powerfully earnest in their attempts to confer dignity upon manual labour that was equal to the intellectual accomplishments of what had come to be known popularly as 'brain work'.[44] Yet there is undoubtedly something overly idealised in the middle-class image of the labourer as man fulfilled by physical work alone. This marriage of physical and mental labour, if noble in its endeavour to raise the working man, seemed bizarre when it was transposed upon the more delicate sensibilities of Oxford undergraduates building roads at Hincksey. Ruskin exhorted the cream of British youth to put down their studies and 'daily to do actually with your hands, something that is useful to mankind'.[45] This proved irresistible to *Punch*, which ruthlessly mocked the project with a poem:

So very Utopian! So Quixotic!
Such is the euphemistic phrase
Equivalent to idiotic
For athletes guided to useful ways ...

> Why shouldn't young Oxford lend hands to Hincksey ...
> Scholars of Ruskin to him be true![46]

The original 'young Oxford', that of the University, had indeed rallied to Ruskin's call.[47] Disappointingly for all involved, not least the poor people of Hincksey, the road built by Ruskin's scholars was appalling.

Given the failure of Ruskin's road making project to provide any real improvement for the poor, and its emphasis on the dignity of labour for a distinctly privileged group of aesthetically minded Oxford undergraduates, it is perhaps curious that the image of Ruskin as road-maker recurs so frequently as a symbol of the newly formed Ruskin Hall. One illustration from *Young Oxford* goes so far as to date the spiritual 'opening' of Ruskin Hall back to the road-mending of 1874, with a brawny Ruskin, arms open in a Christ-like gesture, welcoming the young men of Oxford to join his promised land of healthy labour.[48]

Plate 2: The reign of law

Source: Young Oxford, Vol.1, No.1, October 1899, p15.

This myth of Ruskin as a physically active champion of labour gave the image a distinctive power at a time when the College was striving to establish some kind of corporate identity. In another illustration, we find the idle and flabby embodiment of middle England, John Bull, listening intently to a diminutive yet animated Ruskin the road-mender.[49]

Plate 3: Young Oxford instructing John Bull concerning life's higher interests

Source: *Young Oxford,* Vol.1, No.4, January 1900, p32.

It is precisely the sense of the small yet active Ruskin taking on the might of unwieldy social institutions that characterises much of this visual symbolism which helped to fashion a distinctive Ruskin Hall identity.

One early advertisement in the *Clarion* touted Ruskin Hall as 'the College for young men of small means'.[50] When *Young Oxford* set out its rationale as the College magazine, it described how 'scholars have analysed the working man, dissected paupers, labelled the toiler a commodity'.[51] The working classes, says the anonymous author of the piece, have been under the microscope of the ruling elite for too long and it is Ruskin Hall which will bring about a sweeping reversal of the social order: 'Though they have dissected and analysed us, they have never yet analysed themselves. That is left for us to do'.[52] Here we witness first hand the examined classes, turning the microscope on their long-time examiners. In the curious accompanying illustration, a group of artisans and artists representing 'the People' is looking down a telescope at a university scholar, whose body has mutated into that of a bug.

Plate 4: *We, the People, are now estimating our relative importance by a new standard, and are classifying scholars as they used to classify us.*

Source: *Young Oxford*, Vol.1, No.1, Oxford 1899, p13.

The cultural historian Michel Foucault has suggested that the process of an empowered bourgeoisie finding labels for the lower orders of society not only isolates and subordinates certain groups and individuals, but also provides points at which they can begin to shape strategies of resistance.[53] In other words, the victimised can take over and control the language and symbolism of the victimiser. Often, the battleground for this struggle for power is located at the body itself. Thus in another startling illustration, the corpse of the People arises from the mortuary slab to wield the scalpel against the bourgeois surgeon: 'We have been the corpse and Scholarship the surgeon long enough. Now *we* are going to use the knife, and let the learned fraternity play corpse awhile'. Much like the creature in Mary Shelley's *Frankenstein*, the rude yet physically powerful minion rises up against his masters.[54]

Plate 5: Since the advent of Ruskin Hall the corpse has arisen, and is now trying its hand on the surgeon. The people are now studying the brain tissues of the learned, and a new science is being born.

Source: Young Oxford, Vol.1, No.1, October 1899, p35.

In a note of ghoulish humour, the working-class cadaver is given a distinctive and anarchic social voice by which to shatter the scholarly rhetoric. We hear the corpse, 'while proceeding to apply the knife', cry, 'Turns about is fair play'.[55]

Plate 6: A specimen of successful university training that Ruskin Hall cannot reproduce

Source: Young Oxford, Vol.1, No.1 October 1899, p31.

The key founding members of Ruskin Hall, despite being privileged men with experience of Oxford University, undeniably held unorthodox views on class and gender politics. The two American founders, Walter Vrooman and Charles Beard, both married economically powerful women who were fighting actively for equality, whilst the first Principal, Dennis Hird, had written a radical pamphlet entitled *Jesus the Socialist* and was also strongly in favour of suffrage. Conscious of this sense of the intellectual and economic diminutiveness of the new college, Vrooman maintained at the opening ceremony that the key to educational success was to establish 'clearly the ideal of manhood or special attitude to be striven for'. Yet the model for Ruskin Hall 'manliness' was not as radical as one might have hoped. As Christian Socialists, Vrooman and Hird defined the ideal of manliness as a balance between the binaries of healthy mind and healthy body. This could be an extremely limiting definition by which a man should conduct his life. Any imbalance was, in this equation between the mental and the physical, readily dismissed as deviant and diseased. Thus the University man is most often represented as a frail and enervated swat, 'debarred from any kind of useful work ... the feeble degenerate into hapless bookworms. Hence the abnormal types that crop up in university towns'.[56] The body of the Oxford Scholar in plate 6 has literally decayed from flesh and blood into paper and ink

In his opening article in *Young Oxford*, Vrooman evokes the Christian Socialist dualities of the 'healthy relation' between body and mind, arguing that 'we find many University Professors and Fellows who are giants of understanding, yet who are feeling and volitional idiots. They are capable of thinking all things, but of doing nothing'. As a further insult, he argues that the ancient Universities were devised 'to train priests wholly in reference to other world interests'.[57] Since the attacks on the Catholic Cardinal Newman by Charles Kingsley in the 1840s, to be a 'priest' was to be both a Papist and a celibate, in other words to be distinctly both un-English and un-manly.[58] Vrooman implies that Oxford University men are effeminate and physically spineless, like 'a human body lacking bones'. One accompanying illustration, entitled '*Young Oxford* restoring comeliness and power to an impotent mass', shows Ruskin the road-mender literally putting the backbone into the flabby body of Oxford scholarship.

Plate 7: *Young Oxford restoring comeliness and power to an impotent mass*

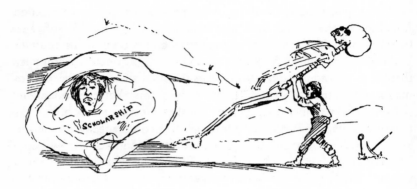

Source: *Young Oxford*, Vol.1. No.1, October 1899, p6.

The face of this 'scholarship' bears a striking resemblance to caricatures of Oscar Wilde as the effeminate aesthete who appeared in *Punch* from the 1880s until after his trial for gross indecency in 1895.[59] The aim of Ruskin Hall, argues Vrooman, is to take scholarship out of the 'paralytic hands' of the effete university man and place it within the brawny grasp of the working-class labour movement.

From 1895, when the trials of Oscar Wilde had made public the link between aestheticism, moral corruption and the newly defined term 'homosexuality', the artistic Oxford intellectual was readily branded a 'degenerate'. The element of Wilde's lifestyle which attracted most censure from the authorities was not the fact that he had engaged in sex with a young aristocratic man, Lord Alfred Douglas, but that he had previously had sex with working-class men. The Oxford aesthete was thus not only a sexual invert but a class traitor in the eyes of upholders of middle-class manliness such as the Christian Socialists.[60] Ironically, this tendency to vilify the aesthete is highly prominent in the writings of the Ruskin Hall men in *Young Oxford*, who championed the words of Max Nordau's infamous work of social definition and segregation, *Degeneration* (1895). 'How many of our intellectual young men there are', Nordau observed, 'who are examples of what are known as Degenerates'.[61] Unfortunately, this line of thinking did much to promote sexual, racial and class intolerance for anyone who did not conform to the rigid laws of the empowered classes.[62] To label the Oxford man as 'degenerate' on account of his heightened sensibility was to limit the possibilities for the self-expression of all men. Wilde, in works sadly overlooked by Ruskin men, such as *The Soul of Man Under Socialism*, had a far finer sympathy for the working man than is demonstrated in any Muscular Christian or imperialist writings.[63] Most ironically of all, he had put his principles into action by working as a road-mender with Ruskin in the spring of 1874.

As Linda Dowling has shown, from the 1850s there had been a conscious project at the University to bring about changes in the curriculum so as to create an 'Oxford-trained elite' capable of running an expanding British Empire.[64] Some Ruskin students were not, unfortunately, immune to these imperialistic sentiments. In a series of shockingly bigoted articles in *Young Oxford*, W.R. Roe likens the non-white races to bacteria which threaten the sound body of the British Empire: 'The Chinese and Negroes gain entrance into our Body Industrial and Body Politic as the bacilli tuberculosis or germs of cancer or blood poisoning gain admittance into the tender flesh of the body human'.[65] Rather than rejecting outright this ruling ideology as the basis of a system of class and racial inequality, Vrooman was at pains to describe himself as 'a citizen of the English-speaking Empire'.[66] The *Manchester Guardian* accused Vrooman of 'meddling as a foreigner' in English education.[67] Cannily, his Opening Day speech was careful to pay heed to the central social concerns of class and Empire:

> ... we come also to present the future leaders of the British Empire an object lesson. Oxford has been sending out its missions and establishing its settlements in the slums. Well, the poor working man is about to make some return. Scholarship can teach the workman many things, but the workman has something to teach scholarship.[68]

Rather than threatening to smash the foundations of Empire, Vrooman reverses the relation between the coloniser and the colonised, arguing that the working-class man may educate the ruling classes.[69] It was a subtle yet bold statement which struck at the very fabric of British society. One early correspondence student described his own undertaking of education as a Herculean task, 'like a man in front of a mountain through which he has to tunnel'.[70] This heroic ideal transferred to the symbolism of the College itself, represented in one illustration as an infant Hercules strangling the old Oxford serpents of scholarly pessimism and naive social optimism.

Plate 8: *The Young (Oxford) Hercules, strangling the serpents, Pessimism and Optimism*

Source: *Young Oxford*, Vol.1, No.3, December 1899, p37.

The college was indeed a male-dominated institution in the early years, creating an identity through what one resident described as 'the binding together' of men in 'a bond of brotherhood'.[71] Yet for all this manly symbolism and talk of the College as a refuge for 'modern monks', Ruskin Hall men were able carve out a life which allowed for vital elements of feminine culture.[72] An early interview with Vrooman documents his desire 'to bring women's gentle influence to bear' on the students through a curriculum of instruction by women teachers, who 'will teach them singing, explain the historical monuments of the city to them, cultivate their moral tone'.[73] Employing women as teachers was simply not the done thing in Oxford Colleges for men. There was an almost hysterical reaction from the *Evening News* when 'four lady members of the Primrose League' were brought into the College not only to 'look after its domestic arrangements', but were also seen to be 'undertaking to deliver a series of lectures on Literature, Art, and Architecture'.[74]

Every student was required to perform at least two hours per day of domestic duties in order to keep running costs to a minimum. The domestic rules of the College were harsh by modern standards, requiring students to be awake by six forty-five every morning.[75] An early flier sent out to advertise the College attempted to confer upon these domestic chores the dignity of manly physical work, by which 'especially industrious young men' could 'support themselves on their own labour'. Vrooman made it clear in his Opening Day address that such domestic work was equal to that of the most manly toil and promised students that there would be no risk of college life 'taking their hard hands and making them soft and white and delicate and tender'.[76] As the one-time tutor in Economics, Sanderson Furniss, remarked, 'the students lived a rather rough life at the college'.[77]

As Hilda Kean has pointed out, 'the male gender role was being challenged in ways students had not expected'.[78] Indeed many commentators, both male and female, found Ruskin Hall life difficult to comprehend. The male correspondent of the *Daily Argos*, careful to emphasise the importance of segregating women from the male scholastic community, remarked upon the need for 'a little settlement of women in another house for the assistance of the hall'.[79] Some male observers were acutely uncomfortable at the sight of grown working men doing domestic duties, and felt unable to watch the students as 'they ply their housewifely trade of washing dishes and preparing the mid-day meal. The visitor's first impulse is to withdraw hastily as from an embarrassing situation'.[80] Yet this anxiety was not confined solely to male visitors. A female correspondent for *The Birkenhead News* 'could not help wishing some good woman could be found to cook for them and look after their small comforts'.[81]

Yet it would be a generalisation to suggest, as Kean does, that 'a new experience of a female domestic world' was always 'unwelcomed' by these men.[82] On the contrary, as the female correspondent for *The Birkenhead News* reported, 'though the residents do not enjoy this part of the programme, they are more than willing to do anything which may bring the long-coveted knowledge within their grasp'.[83] One resident student, F. Fox, was proud of 'our womanless home' because 'it gives us an insight into the work that is done by the average English woman to-day'.[84] The photographic evidence suggests that men performed their duties seriously, and there are many accounts which suggest that the performing of domestic duties actually did enlighten men to some degree as to the conditions endured by women across the country.

Plate 9: Domestic duties at Ruskin college.

Source: Ruskin College Archive

Jack Lawson, in his patriarchally named autobiography *A Man's Life*, recounts how in 1907 'his wife was working in domestic service, and I was combining study with some domestic service in College'. As he goes on to recount,

> At the weekend you put on an apron, took a bucket of water, soap, and scrubbing-brush, and thoroughly scrubbed ... The Scrub List was just as important as the Lecture List – and its educational value was not less ... It was a great experience, an amazing experiment, and amazingly successful.[85]

We should be wary of diminishing the hardships endured by working-class women in daily domestic labour, and undoubtedly these men found the chores an amusing novelty in a way which women could not. Yet we should also be aware of the hardships, and physical dangers, which working men had endured in their daily lives. As Lawson bluntly puts it, the two hours of domestic work 'was like child's play compared with my work in the mine'.[86] *Young Oxford* did at least provide a forum for women, if somewhat infrequently, to speak out on such matters. In one article entitled 'A Woman Hits Back', a female visitor to Ruskin Hall expresses her delight at seeing men performing domestic tasks: 'I think joyously that thereby the labour of at least one woman has been set free ... that what one woman alone is thought to be able to do easily, twenty-five men may come to do'. With no little irony she goes on to add that it is a scheme 'which may even add a new virtue, humility, to the masculine soul and teach them to set bounds to the exactions of domestic life'.[87]

From the outset, Ruskin Hall had championed itself as 'The People's University' which 'offers to every man, woman, and child an opportunity of gaining a complete education'.[88] The first constitution of the College set out to provide for all 'students, whether men or women'.[89] In his autobiography, Sanderson Furniss notes that in October 1899 'the College ... contained fifty students, all men. It had been intended by the founders that both men and women should be provided for, but so far it had not been found practicable to include women students'.[90] This is ironic, given that almost the entire funding for the first year came from the personal fortune of Mrs Amne L. Vrooman, who wrote in *Young Oxford* of her ideal that one day 'women of divergent classes can come together under the same roof to live their life in common, sharing without regard to social caste'.[91] But the combination of domestic duties, lack of funding and society's biased views on education meant that women were simply unable to find the means to come to Ruskin Hall. As one female correspondence student lamented, 'But oh, for a month or two of Ruskin Hall! Women cannot get to that sort of thing so easily as men can: certainly women with home duties, as yet'.[92] It was not until after World War One that women students were finally able to come into residence at Ruskin College.

This was another instance in which the naming of the College after John Ruskin was somewhat problematical. Ruskin himself had what might be described, at best, as a troubled relationship with women, both in theory and in practice. His *Sesame and Lilies* urged women to conform to the role of the household nun through 'modesty of service' and 'self-renunciation', while his fantasies of Medusa-like women in *The Queen of the Air* verge on the misogynistic.[93] In one particularly vivid nightmare of 1869, Ruskin 'dreamed of a serpent with a woman's breasts which entered his room under a door; and another which fastened itself on his neck like a leech'.[94] This psychological excess seems to have been borne out in his real life relationships. Ruskin's marriage to Effie Gray was never consummated on account of his shock at the horrors of her 'period' and 'the notorious first sight of pubic hair'.[95] As Effie recounted, 'he had imagined women were quite different to what he saw I was, and ... the reason he did not make me his wife was because he was disgusted with my person'.[96] Ruskin then became fixated upon a child called Rose La Touche, whose name came to symbolise all that he found repulsive in women – 'Rose and cankerworm ... the one *never* separate from the other'.[97] Effie went on to have eight children by the artist John Everett Millais, but Rose fared much worse, slipping into mental decline.

One Ruskin student, writing in 1900, perceptibly picked up on this strain of inequality in Ruskin's writing, observing that 'in denying a woman the scope of her natural aptitudes and mental ability Ruskin denied her humanity'.[98] But the early attitude towards women at the College fell in practice some way short of the ideal. A ticket for the Opening Day at the Town Hall, on 22 February 1899, contains the telling line: 'One corner specially reserved for ladies'. Indeed, women were often regarded with the same angry contempt as the bourgeoisie in the early years of the College. As one Ruskin man wrote of the University Extension Movement, 'it is essentially a middle-class movement, tending strongly toward a woman's movement, and its very fitness for this work explains its failure to reach the working man'.[99] Lamentably, even by 1913 it was possible for *The Times* to observe that 'no attempt has been made so far to give effect to the clause of the Charter which provides for the inclusion of working women'.[100] Yet some male students were deeply sympathetic to the cause of women, as is shown in this poem by Gerald Massey:

> Our Coming Queen must be the wife of heaven
> The wife who will not wear her bonds with pride
> As adult doll with fripperies glorified:
> The mother fashioned on a nobler plan
> Than woman who was merely made *from* man.[101]

This desire for a degree of female autonomy is in stark contrast to the views of John Ruskin himself. The editors of the College magazine were receptive always to comments on the Woman Question. One female correspondent was highly laudatory of *Young Oxford*'s attacks on traditional male bastions of privilege and praises the publication because it does not 'succumb to the temptation to turn your pencil against women'.[102] Indeed, the tone was increasingly one of optimism for the plight of female workers in society, heralding in the equality of the twentieth-century woman who 'in a desire for knowledge, leaves her washing of clothes and scrubbing of doorsteps to look upon the pages of universal history'.[103]

Despite all of the cultural tensions which I have outlined, as Ruskin Hall attempted to create a permanent class and gender identity in the face of overwhelming social and economic difficulties, the degree of enthusiasm for the College amongst the students remained uniformly and impressively immense. Having inspected the College in detail, the 1913 Board of Education concluded that 'Ruskin College has thrown new light on the educational possibilities of industrial society'; and it would be wise for today's educators and government alike to pay careful heed to this statement.[104] As one *Young Oxford* commentator optimistically put it, 'it is scarcely possible to spend too much on education.'[105] The *Oxford and District Echo*'s salute to Ruskin Hall – 'Hail, oh hail thou harbinger of the millennium' – undoubtedly draws our attention to the present end-of-millennium prospects of Ruskin College.[106] It is difficult for anyone who has recently been involved in adult education not to feel a sense of foreboding at present changes in economic support from a government which has become dulled to its own historical struggle for existence. In the words of George Bernard Shaw, who so feared the detrimental effects of education in Oxford on the working classes, 'I may be wrong. I hope I am'.[107]

The illustrations in this piece were reproduced by kind permission of Ruskin College, with special thanks to David Horsfield and the library staff, and Bill Dewhurst.

NOTES

1. Walter Vrooman, 'Modern Scholarship', *Young Oxford: A Monthly Magazine Devoted to the Ruskin Hall Movement*, Vol.1, No.1, October 1899, p5.
2. *The West End*, 31 May 1899, p551.
3. 'To the Builders of Branch Colleges', *Young Oxford*, Vol.1, No.3, December 1899, p13.
4. 'The University Don: A Letter from a Ruskin Hall Student who is earning his way through college entirely by his own industry', *Young Oxford*, vol.1, no.3, December 1899, p8.
5. For an overview of the College in its early years see Harold Pollins, *The History of Ruskin College*, Ruskin College Library Publication, no.3, Oxford 1984, pp9-27. A more detailed account is given in Paul Yorke, *Education and the Working Class: Ruskin College, 1899-1909*, Ruskin Students Labour History Pamphlets, no.1, Oxford 1977.

6. Buxton was the father of the former Vice-Principal and a President of the Board of Trade. Reported in *The Oxford Times*, 10 February 1912, p30.

7. Brian Simon, *Education and the Labour Movement, 1870-1920: Studies in the History of Education*, Lawrence and Wishart, London 1965, p312.

8. *The Oxford Times*, 10 February 1912, p30. For a brief account of the 1909 Student Strike see Bernard Jennings, 'Revolting Students – the Ruskin College Dispute 1908-9', *Studies in Adult Education*, vol.9, no.1, 1977, pp1-16.

9. *The Sketch*, 22 February 1899, p204.

10. 'A Ruskin Hall at Oxford. Munificent Gift', *Manchester Guardian*, 9 December 1899.

11. 'A Oxford gli studenti dell' Università (la vera) tennero dei *meetings* per avvisare ai modi di incoraggiarlo, prestandovi l'opera loro', *Gazzetta del Popolo*, no.114, Turin, 24 April 1899. My translation.

12. Edmund Stonelake, *The Autobiography of Edmund Stonelake*, Educational Committee Publication, Mid-Glamorgan 1981, p75.

13. Letter from George Bernard Shaw to Charles Beard, 1 May 1899, Ruskin College Archive.

14. E. Traynor, 'A Farewell Trip up the River', *Young Oxford*, vol.2, no.14, November 1900, p58.

15. W.W. Craik, *The Central Labour College, 1909-29: a Chapter in the History of Working-Class Education*, Lawrence and Wishart, London 1964, p68.

16. *Oxford Review*, 11 March 1899.

17. *The St. James's Gazette*, 23 February 1899.

18. *Young Oxford*, vol.1, no.3, December 1899, p33.

19. Letter from Herbert Spencer, Brighton, 11 February 1899, Ruskin College Archive.

20. For an account of these figures in the moulding of Victorian masculinity, see Richard Dellamora, *Masculine Desire: The Sexual Politics of Victorian Aestheticism*, University of North Carolina Press, Chapel Hill and London 1990.

21. *Punch*, 15 February 1899.

22. Jack Lawson, *A Man's Life*, Hodder & Stoughton Ltd, London 1944, p102.

23. *Ibid.*, p102.

24. Stonelake, *op.cit.*, p74.

25. 'A Graveyard for Agitators', *Young Oxford*, vol.1, no.1, October 1899, p20.

26. *Young Oxford*, vol.1, no.3, December 1899, p33.

27. Frank Merry, 'How to Start a Branch at Ruskin Hall', *Young Oxford*, vol.1, no.2, November 1899, p10.

28. 'Short Prospectus of Courses of Instruction at Ruskin Hall, Oxford, 1899', Ruskin College Archive.

29. 'Ruskin Hall Opened', *The Clarion*, 4 March 1899.

30. Walter Vrooman, 'Modern Scholarship', *Young Oxford*: vol.1, no.1, October, 1899, p1.

31. 'Such a Sphinx is this Life of ours, to all men and all societies of men. Nature, like the Sphinx, is of womanly celestial loveliness and tenderness; the face and bosom of a goddess, but ending in claws and the body of a lioness. There is in her a celestial beauty – which means celestial order, pliancy to wisdom; but there is also a darkness, a ferocity, fatality, which are infernal. She is a goddess, but one yet not disimprisoned; one still half-imprisoned – the articulate, lovely, still encased in the inarticulate, chaotic'. Thomas Carlyle, *Past and Present* (1843), in H.D. Traill (ed), *The Works of Thomas Carlyle*, vol.X, Macmillan, London 1899, p7.

32. *Oxford Times*, 25 February 1899.

33. 'In Memory of John Ruskin', *Young Oxford*, vol.1, no.5, February 1900, p13.

34. P.D. Anthony, *John Ruskin's Labour: A Study of Ruskin's Social Theory*, Cambridge University Press, Cambridge 1983, p104.

35. Joan Evans, *John Ruskin*, Jonathan Cape, London 1954, p407.

36. 'Short Prospectus of Courses of Instruction at Ruskin Hall, Oxford, 1899', Ruskin College Archive. My italics.

37. Charles Beard seems at pains to stress that it was Ruskin the social critic, not the artist, after whom the College was named, in 'Ruskin and the Babble of Tongues', *New Republic*, 5 August 1936, p372.

38. For an account of this see John Dixon Hunt, *The Wider Sea: A Life of John Ruskin*, Viking Press, New York 1982, p34.

39. John Ruskin, in E. T. Cook and Alexander Wedderburn (eds), *The Works of John Ruskin*, vol.XX, G. Allen, London 1903-12, pxii.

40. For an overview of this ideal of *mens sana in corpore sano*, see Bruce Haley, *The Healthy Body and Victorian Culture*, Harvard University Press, Cambridge 1978, pp23-68.

41. Donald E. Hall, 'Muscular Christianity: Reading and Writing the Male Social Body', in Donald E. Hall (ed.), *Muscular Christianity: Embodying the Victorian Age*, Cambridge University Press, Cambridge 1994, pp3-16, p7. For a detailed account of Christian Socialism, see Norman Vance, *The Sinews of the Spirit: The Ideal of Christian Manliness in Victorian Literature and Religious Thought*, Cambridge University Press, Cambridge 1985.

42. Derrick Leon sees the 1854 college as 'an attempt to produce, through an affectional link between the master and labouring classes, a new type of

social democracy based upon mutual respect and understanding, culture, order and goodwill', in *Ruskin: The Great Victorian*, Routledge & Keegan Paul, London 1949, p226. On the other hand, Patrick Brantlinger regards the College as embodying the desire of the ruling classes to 'impose intelligent order on those who seem disorderly, unintelligent, "primitive" or "savage", creatures of darkness', in *The Spirit of Reform: British Literature and Politics, 1832-1867*, Cornell University Press, Ithaca, NY 1988, p254.

43. John Ruskin, *Munera Pulveris*, in *Works, op.cit.*, vol.XVII, p232.

44. Ford Madox Brown's famous painting *Work* also attempted unsuccessfully to reconcile physical and intellectual labour. As Herbert Sussman points out, in the painting Thomas Carlyle 'is rather notoriously represented watching from the sidelines as muscular, idealised navvies do the heavy digging'. As Sussman goes on to argue, 'Carlyle shared Brown's middle-class jealousy of what seemed the untroubled masculinity, the "happiness" of the working class so clearly manifested in their evident delight for muscular work, a form of class-bound muscle envy that runs throughout the century, as in Ruskin's road-building experiment at Oxford', in *Victorian Masculinities: Manhood and Masculine Poetics in Early Victorian Literature and Art*, Cambridge University Press, Cambridge 1995, pp39-41.

45. John Ruskin, 'Imagination', *Aratra Pentelici*, in *Works, op cit.*, vol.xxiii, pixiv.

46. *Punch*, 6 June 1874.

47. Harold Pollins rightly notes that the magazine *Young Oxford* was named 'as though to distinguish it from the old' (*op.cit.*, p10). Yet the term has more telling resonance in that it had long existed in the University itself as a reappropriation of the Disraelian term 'Young England', coined by Thomas Hughes in *Tom Brown's Schooldays* as an ideal of corporate, bourgeois manliness.

48. *Young Oxford*, vol.1, no.1, October 1899, p15.

49. *Ibid.*, p32.

50. *Clarion*, 14 January 1899.

51. 'Wanted: Helpers for Scientific Research', *Young Oxford*, vol.1, no.1, October 1899, p14.

52. *Ibid.*, p14.

53. Michel Foucault, *The History of Sexuality, Volume 1: An Introduction* [1976], trans. Robert Hurley, Random House, Vintage Books, New York 1980, pp100-2.

54. The portrayal of the working classes, and supposedly 'inferior' races, like the Irish, as Frankenstein's 'monster' was common in middle-class publications such as *Punch*. See L. Perry Curtis, *Apes and Angels: The Irishman*

in Victorian Literature, revised edition, Smithsonian Institution Press, Washington and London 1997.

55. *Young Oxford*, vol.1, no.1, October 1899, p14.
56. 'A Life-long Student', *Young Oxford*, vol.1, no.4, January 1900, p36.
57. *Young Oxford*, vol.1, no.1, October 1899, p4.
58. See Alan Sinfield, *The Wilde Century: Effeminacy, Oscar Wilde and the Queer Moment*, Cassell, London 1994.
59. For a general discussion of the symbolism of Wilde's body, see Ed Cohen, *Talk on the Wilde Side: Toward a Genealogy of a Discourse on Male Sexualities*, Routledge, New York & London 1993. For a discussion of how contemporary representations of Wilde's body changed after his arrest, see Nick Kneale, 'The Scent for Perversion: Nasal Myths and Fictions in the Later Nineteenth Century', in Lene Oestermark and Victoria de Rijlke (eds), *Reading the Nose*, Middlesex University Press, London 1999.
60. 'Aestheticism' may be briefly defined as the detaching of art from all morality, as expressed in the phrase 'Art for Art's Sake'. Ruskin Hall students supplanted the motto with their own version: '"Art for Art's Sake" is merely a degenerate vapouring born of a diseased system of social parasitism ... "Art for Life's sake" is the only true principle'. Robert Gardner, 'The Brains of Democracy. IV. Labour & Art', *Young Oxford*, vol.3, no.25, October 1901, p292.
61. Nordau, quoted in *Young Oxford*, vol.1, no.1, October 1899, p11.
62. William Greenslade has commented on how degeneration theory 'naturalises' anxieties about class, race and gender 'into a biological fact'. See *Degeneration, Culture and the Novel 1880-1940*, Cambridge University Press, Cambridge 1994, p23.
63. 'In the modern stress of competition and struggle for place, such sympathy is naturally rare, and is also very much stifled by the immoral ideal of uniformity of type and conformity to rule which is so prevalent everywhere, and is perhaps most obnoxious in England'. Oscar Wilde, 'The Soul of Man Under Socialism' in *De Profundis and Other Writings*, Penguin, London 1973, p50.
64. Linda Dowling, *Hellenism and Homosexuality in Victorian Oxford*, Cornell University Press, Ithaca and London 1994, p72.
65. 'The Race Problem by an Imperial Socialist', *Young Oxford*, vol.2, no.20, May 1901, p280.
66. *Oxford Times*, 25 February 1899.
67. 'An Experiment in Education', *The Manchester Guardian*, 23 February 1899.
68. 'A Labour College for Oxford', *Oxford Times*, 14 January 1899, p9. This

is a reprint of an interview originally given by Vrooman to the *Daily Telegraph*.

69. For more on the concept of 'reverse colonisation' at this time, with special reference to Bram Stoker's *Dracula* (1897), see Stephen Arata, *Fictions of Loss in the Victorian Fin de Siècle*, Cambridge University Press, Cambridge 1996, chapter 5. See also my discussion of Arata's concept, 'in which the primitive victim encroaches upon the territory of the civilised victimizer', in 'Review', *Modern Language Review*, 93.4, October 1998, pp1092-3.

70. 'Some Friendly Letters', *Young Oxford*, vol.1, no.1, October 1899, p29.

71. 'The Ruskin Hall Fraternal League', *Young Oxford*, vol.1, no.10, July 1900, pp22-4. For the seminal theory on male bonding in Western culture, see Eve Kosofsky Sedgwick, *Between Men: English Literature and Male Homosocial Desire*, Columbia University Press, New York 1985.

72. George E. Griffiths, 'Characteristics of Ruskin Hall Men', *Young Oxford* vol.1, no.11, August 1900, pp19-20.

73. *Oxford and District Morning Echo*, 9 January 1899.

74. 'Primrose Dames as Professors', *Evening News*, 6 April 1899.

75. 'Regulations for the Domestic Organization of Ruskin Hall', 3 January 1902.

76. *Birmingham and District Trades Journal*, 11 March 1899.

77. Henry Sanderson Furniss [Lord Sanderson], *Memories of Sixty Years*, Methuen & Co. Ltd, London 1931, p87.

78. Hilda Kean, 'Myths of Ruskin College', *Studies in the Education of Adults*, vol.28, no.2, October 1996, pp211-223, p214.

79. *Daily Argos*, 29 February 1899.

80. *The West End*, 31 May 1899, p552.

81. 'Ruskin Hall, Oxford (from a Lady Correspondent)', *Oxford Chronicle*, 12 August 1899.

82. Hilda Kean, *op.cit.*, p214.

83. 'Ruskin Hall, Oxford (from a Lady Correspondent)', *Oxford Chronicle*, 12 August 1899.

84. F. Fox, 'Domestic Life at Ruskin Hall', *Young Oxford*, vol.2, no.13, October 1900, p16.

85. Jack Lawson, *A Man's Life*, Hodder & Stoughton Ltd, London 1944, p99.

86. *Ibid.*, p100.

87. 'A Woman Hits Back', *Young Oxford*, vol.1, no.1, October 1899, p23.

88. 'Souvenir of the Visit of the Oldham Co-operators to Ruskin Hall, Oxford, Sat 9 June 1900', Ruskin College Archive.

89. 'Memorandum and Articles of Association of Ruskin Hall Incorporated, 11 June 1900', Ruskin College Archive.

90. Sanderson Furniss, *op.cit.*, p86.
91. 'A Ruskin Hall for Women', *Young Oxford*, vol.1, no.7, April 1900, p12.
92. *Young Oxford*, vol.1, no.9, June 1900, p32.
93. John Ruskin, *Sesame and Lilies*, J.M. Dent, London 1970, p60. For a survey of representations of women at the time see Bram Dijkstra, *Idols of Perversity: Fantasies of Feminine Evil in Fin-de-Siècle Culture*, Oxford University Press, Oxford 1986.
94. Van Akin Burd, *John Ruskin and Rose La Touche: Her Unpublished Diaries of 1861 and 1867*, Clarendon Press, Oxford 1979, p119.
95. John Dixon Hunt, *op.cit.*, p175.
96. Tim Hilton, *John Ruskin: The Early Years 1819-59*, Yale University Press, New Haven 1985, p48.
97. John Ruskin, 'The Hesperid Aeglé', *Works*, *op.cit.*, vol VII, p422.
98. N.G. Bacon, 'Ruskin on Woman and Education', *Young Oxford*, vol.2, no.14, November 1900, p43.
99. 'Extension Old and New', *Young Oxford*, vol.1, no.1, October 1899, p11.
100. 'Ruskin College, Oxford. History and Development', *The Times*, 21 February, 1913.
101. *Young Oxford*, vol.1, no.3, December 1899, p28.
102. Letter signed 'Old Maid', Manchester, 1 November 1899. Ruskin College Archive.
103. 'The Twentieth-century Woman, Looking Around and Backward', *Young Oxford*, vol.2, no.15, December 1900, p100.
104. Board of Education, 'Report of an Inspection of Ruskin College, Oxford, held on 21-26 April, 1913', p18. Ruskin College Archive. Whilst stressing the huge advances made since the founding of the College, the Board still recommended that first year students 'need help in the formation of new habits of mind and body', while second years needed 'to seek points of contact with the best and broadest influences of the University'.
105. 'A Co-operative University', *Young Oxford*, vol.1, no.2, November 1899, p20.
106. *Oxford and District Morning Echo*, 12 December, 1898.
107. Letter from George Bernard Shaw to Charles Beard, 1 May 1899. Ruskin College Archive.

The 1908 Report:
Antidote to Class Struggle?

ROGER FIELDHOUSE

At the beginning of this century there was a groundswell of support for more educational opportunities for the working class, and in 1907 a conference took place in Oxford in support of such opportunities. The conference called for more places for working-class men at institutions of higher education. Partly in response to this, the government commissioned a report into working class education, and into the role that the university might take in such education. Ruskin College was a collaborator in the Report, which was entitled *Oxford and Working-class Education*.

In one of its most famous and most frequently quoted passages, *Oxford and Working-class Education* incontrovertibly asserts that it had always been the older universities' privilege 'to train men for all departments of political life and public administration' (para 78). It was echoing James Stuart's argument, thirty-seven years earlier, that Cambridge University should extend 'the benefits of the University throughout the country' in order to 'continue in its hands the permeating influence which it is desirable that it should possess'.[1] According to the 1908 Report, it was 'incumbent upon universities to watch carefully every sign that a new class is ready to receive their guidance' (para 83). They argued that current circumstances made it imperative that the working classes 'should obtain the knowledge necessary to enable them to show foresight in their choice of political means' (paras 77–78). The timing and the content of the Report should thus be seen in the context of the developments within the labour movement and the spread of socialist ideas in Britain within the preceding quarter century.

During the 1850s and 1860s a respectable 'new model' trade union movement had opted to collaborate with employers in the expectation that this would entitle them to share in the bonanza of the 'golden age of British capitalism'. For the labour aristocrats of the craft unions at least, this strategy did apparently yield huge dividends in the form of improved standards of living, political enfranchisement, trade union rights and a mass of social reform legislation, in return for their unaggressive, conciliatory approach to industrial relations. By the early 1870s they had obtained apparently unending prosperity and 'a wholly unexpected place in the sun.'[2] But economic depression in the later 1870s meant that there was no longer the continuous growth to provide full employment and constantly rising real wages, even for the labour aristocracy. They discovered that sliding scales could go down as well as up and that labour was still a disposable asset in a capitalist economy – to be discarded when no longer needed. The new model unions faced defeats and decline as their members struggled with the consequences of structural changes in industry. Shrinking profit margins forced firms to merge or amalgamate in search of economies of scale and introduce mechanisation which caused job losses and de-skilling. 'Step by step the labour aristocrat found himself forced into the ranks of the working class; and, on the whole, he moved to the left'.[3] It was in this industrial and political atmosphere that Britain witnessed the emergence of socialist organisations and ideas and a 'new unionism' during the 1880s.[4]

In 1881 the Democratic Federation was founded by H.M. Hyndman and by 1884, when it changed its name to the Social Democratic Federation (SDF), it had become a focus of working-class revolutionism, at least in London. It quickly grew into 'the first modern socialist organisation of national importance in Britain'.[5] A breakaway from the SDF led by William Morris and Eleanor Marx formed the Socialist League in 1884. Although it succumbed to anarchism after a few years, the Socialist League was important in spreading more libertarian, less deterministic notions of socialism than those favoured by Hyndman and the SDF. While neither organisation attracted a mass membership, their appearance signified the introduction of organised Marxism in this country. During 1886 and 1887 London experienced a spate of socialist demonstrations organised by the League and the SDF, giving rise to rumours and fears of insurrection, and violent clashes with the police and troops.

Meanwhile, the Home Rule crisis of 1885–86 split the Liberal Party and opened the way to the formation of an independent, working-class Labour Party. Already, in 1884, the Fabian Society had been founded. Although clearly not a working-class organisation, it was advocating a transition to a socialist society through increasing state intervention and municipal enterprise – what became known as 'gas and water socialism'. This evolutionary socialism was not widely regarded as a serious threat to existing social structures, but it was seen by the bourgeoisie as a move in the wrong direction. Their apprehension was heightened in 1888 by Keir Hardie's Mid-Lanark by-election campaign which was a signal of the beginning of the 'labour revolt' against the domination of the Liberal Associations.'[6]

More immediately significant, and threatening, was a revival of militancy amongst trade unionists. Between 1886–88, iron and steel workers railway workers and miners formed new, more militant unions – the British Steel Smelters' Amalgamated Association, the Amalgamated Society of Railway Servants and the Miners' Federation of Great Britain. Other craftsmen, such as building workers and engineers, were likewise showing greater militancy; but it was the successful unionisation of the previously unorganised 'labouring poor' that made the 'new unionism' seem really threatening. The invasion of Westminster by the striking match girls and women in 1888, and the victorious dockers' strike of 1889, with the subsequent formation of general labour unions – to unite workers on a class, rather than a sectional, basis – raised the spectre of mass working-class organisation. By 1889 there were approximately three-quarters of a million trade unionists in Britain. This trade union explosion 'provided the opportunity for socialists to move away from merely propagandist work, or from the quasi-insurrectionary fantasies of unemployed riots, into the potentially much more fruitful area of strike leadership and trade union activity.'[7] As Engels put it, 'the masses are on the move and there is no holding them any more.'[8]

Within three or four years, this new unionism was in retreat before a counter-attack by the employers, and the union membership among unskilled workers rapidly declined. But it did survive in expanding industries, such as water, gas and electricity. More important, the division between old and new unionism, craftsmen and unskilled workers, was disappearing. Faced by an onslaught on trade unionism by employers, judiciary and government, all trade unionists began to feel a common identity. Moreover, there was a drawing together of this new unionism and the political activists. 'There was a natural affinity between the ethos of new unionism, with its emphasis on working-class solidarity and support for state action, and the ideals of the socialists'.[9]

Radicalism had been spreading in London for some years, stimulated by Bradlaugh's secularist campaign; the agitation for electoral reform in 1884 and Home Rule after 1886; and Fabian 'municipal socialism', especially after the formation of the London County Council in 1888. In the provinces a more specifically *socialist* independence from the two major political parties was being fomented by the *Clarion* (an influential and popular socialist newspaper launched in Manchester by Robert Blatchford in 1891, which succeeded in spreading socialist ideas amongst the working class); and this was supported by the labour and socialist clubs that sprang up in the industrial West Riding and Lancashire during the 1890s. This new political force was given considerable impetus by the return of Keir Hardie, John Burns and Havelock Wilson as independent labour candidates for West Ham, Battersea and Middlesbrough in the 1892 general election.

Even more significant was the formation in the following year of the Independent Labour Party (ILP), which aimed to weld the trade union and political wings of the growing labour movement together. The ILP, which was founded at a meeting in Bradford, reflected particularly the provincial independence from the main political parties and had a much stronger working-class base than the Fabian Society. It offered an evangelical socialist crusade against the evils of capitalism, with the object of establishing a classless, harmonious socialist commonwealth where competition would be replaced by co-operation, conflict by fellowship and hierarchy by equality. Its first priority was to secure the election of independent Labour men to Parliament rather than fight the class war and it therefore adopted a programme of social reform rather than all-out socialism, in order to appeal to a wider electorate and avoid antagonising the unions. Nevertheless, despite this moderation, its socialist objective – to secure the collective ownership of the means of production, distribution and exchange – and its widespread working-class support, were enough to cause alarm amongst middle-class Conservatives and Liberals.

The ILP made progress in local government elections. By 1900 it claimed 106 local councillors, 66 members of school boards and 51 poor law guardians. This progress, and that of the Fabians, was not without its set-backs, but, together with the SDF, they gradually increased the number of Labour members serving on borough councils during the 1890s. By 1895 there were approximately 600 Labour councillors and in 1898 West Ham became the first local council to have a Labour majority.

There was little the ruling class could do about this constitutional progress, but attempts could be, and were, made to halt the advance of the new unionism. Vigorous policing helped to break the gasworkers' strike in 1889 and the use of police baton charges, troops, cavalry and even warships became a feature of industrial disputes during the 1890s. At Featherstone in 1893 two locked-out miners were shot dead and a number of others wounded when soldiers opened fire on a demonstration. Anti-union propaganda was also used, particularly in effective newspaper presentation of the employers' attack on the unions as a battle of 'free labour' against the coercion of the unions and the corporate tyranny of the closed shop. Employers' organisations, such as the Shipping Federation, were used to recruit and transport black-leg labour to break strikes. In 1893 several thousand 'free labourers' were brought to Hull under military and police protection for this purpose. In the same year a National Free Labour Association was formed to supply employers with workmen wherever there was a strike. In 1896 the Engineering Employers' Federation declared the employers' determination to obtain the freedom to manage their own affairs and to adopt an American-style union-smashing policy. The following year it instigated a selective national lockout of members of the Amalgamated Soeiety of Engineers – virtually forcing them to abandon all collective bargaining, resistance to piecework and demands for the closed shop. 'The defeat of the aristocratic engineers sent a shock wave of insecurity through the whole trade union movement.'[10]

Not content with this onslaught, the judiciary mounted an attack on the trade union immunities granted in legislation of 1871 and 1875. A judgement of 1896 found that putting pressure on people to deter them from entering their place of work was illegal – thus outlawing what previously had been considered legitimate peaceful picketing. And five years later, in 1901, the famous Taff Vale case found the Amalgamated Society of Railway Servants liable for losses sustained by the railway company during a strike. This judgement, combined with another, two weeks later, which stated that a strike, or even a threat to strike, could be considered a conspiracy to injure, rendered the unions liable for damages caused by any industrial action and effectively paralysed them.

In the face of these attacks, there was growing support in the trade union movement for the strengthening of Labour representation in Parliament, to look after its interests and seek protective trade union legislation. Since the Liberal Party's disastrous showing in the 1895 general election, there was increasing enthusiasm for the idea of an independent, working-class political party. In February 1900 a conference of trade unions, the Fabian Society, the ILP and SDF agreed to establish a distinct Labour group in Parliament. A Labour Representation Committee (LRC), consisting of two members of the ILP, two from the SDF, one Fabian and seven trade unionists, was authorised to run independent Labour candidates. At first, progress was slow but the Taff Vale judgement galvanished the trade unions into support.

In 1902 David Shackleton won a by-election at Clitheroe as an LRC candidate and he was joined the following year by Will Crooks who was elected for Woolwich and Arthur Henderson for Barnard Castle. By 1903, the year which also saw the formation of the Workers' Educational Association (WEA), the LRC had close on one million members and had become a potentially powerful party in its own right. The Liberals therefore sought an electoral pact with the LRC, to incorporate them into a Liberal alliance before they became a real threat. As a result of this pact, 29 LRC candidates were elected in the 1906 general election. With one other member subsequently joining the newly-named Labour Party, it boasted 30 members when Parliament reassembled in February 1906. 'The rather synthetic' Tory horror at the 'socialist' advance[11] undoubtedly exaggerated the socialism of the new party, but was not altogether feigned. The real reason for the fear of the middle or ruling classes was not the emergent labour movement's extreme socialism – its predominant ideology was much closer to liberalism with a collectivist tinge – but its *mass* appeal, its distinctly working-class constituency and its apparent independence of the guiding tutelage of the bourgeoisie. For them, as the 1908 Report makes clear, this redistribution of political power made it vital that the working class (and particularly its leaders) should receive such guidance.

This seemed all the more urgent because at its periphery the labour movement was not liberal-collectivist: it was opening the door to Marxism. 'By 1900 the SDF had established itself as a national force with some 43 branches in London alone. Forthright SDF propaganda had made socialism a vital force influencing many thousands of workers'.[12] In 1903 a Scottish group broke away from the SDF, consisting of 'impossibilists' who opposed the SDF's reformist compromises, flirtations with parliamentary politics and any short-term palliatives on the road to socialism. They formed a separate Socialist Labour Party (SLP) and the following year a London-based breakaway from the SDF formed the Socialist Party of Great Britian (SPGB). The SLP and SPGB were Bolshevik-type revolutionary parties, convinced that socialism would arrive only after the collapse of capitalism and would be achieved only by a well-disciplined, ideologically sound cadre of revolutionaries who would lead the workers in the class struggle when the time came. They argued 'the need to create a new type of working-class party, one that could act as a vanguard, providing the most dedicated, self-sacrificing and knowledgeable people for the class battles ... [The SLP] came to see that the capitalist state could not be gradually transformed into a socialist one; that the capitalist state had to be smashed and replaced by a workers' state. It also saw that, to accomplish the execution of capitalism, a sharp knife – namely, a revolutionary party – was required.'[13] The SLP also favoured general industrial unions (in opposition to the liberal-reformist, sectional craft unions) and in 1906 founded the 'Advocates of Industrial Unionism', whose ultimate aim was stated in the SLP paper, *The Socialist*, in April 1908: '... having overthrown the class state the united Industrial Unions will furnish the administrative machinery for directing industry in the Socialist Commonwealth'.[14]

Although the membership of these revolutionary parties was very small numerically (and purposely restricted to ideological purists), their influence cannot be measured in terms of membership figures. They took a very prominent part in the politicisation of the labour movement after 1900 and they helped to stimulate 'the proliferation of revolutionary industrial organisations'[15] which led to the outbreak of syndicalism amongst trade unionists (even though the SLP opposed pure syndicalism which denied the role of a revolutionary party). 'Although only briefly a force of consequence, syndicalism ... had a lasting influence on the development of the British labour movement. It was a nursery school, a training ground for militants'.[16]

Thus by the early twentieth century there was 'a socialist movement, a Marxist tradition, a challenge from the socialists to the old line liberal leaders in the unions and with the LRC the first signs of the emergence of organised labour as an independent political force.'[17] Conscious of the growing strength of the socialist parties in Germany and France, British Liberals as well as Conservatives were anxious to prevent the same thing happening in this country.

One of the problems they had to overcome was the spread of independent working-class education which was helping to equip the socialist movement with the intellectual tools to challenge the liberal ideology. By the end of the nineteenth century, militant activists in the labour movement were finding themselves in need of the education they had been denied at school particularly in such subjects as economics, politics, history, and sociology. But 'because of their angle of interest, many workers who wanted to study held a deep suspicion of "expert" advice and educational "uplift" '[18] such as that offered by the Adult Schools or University Extension, soon to be imitated by the WEA. There was already a strong independent working-class autodidactic tradition, typified by such men as John Burns, Tom Mann and Tommy Jackson. This tradition was radical rather than socialist or Marxist, but it was subversive and disruptive and the autodidacts learnt a great deal about exploitation and the class struggle. Even more important, they controlled both the process and the content of their education: 'it remained *their* education, for they defined both the purpose and the boundaries of their intellectual exploration'.[19] To this tradition was now added a network of study groups, study circles and classes organised by the socialist movement which produced its own tutors. The Clarion movement, the Co-operative movement, the Labour Church movement, the Socialist Sunday Schools, the SDF, the Socialist League, the Fabian Society and the ILP were all part of 'a whole complex of institutions reflecting the outlook of the working class and under their own control' which set out, in the words of the Socialist League slogan, to 'educate, agitate, organise'[20] and 'paved the way for a rebirth of the idea of independent working-class education.'[21] For example, Hyndman's books popularising Marxian economics stimulated an interest in learning about alternatives to orthodox political economy. The Fabian Society provided book boxes and organised classes in economics, history, local government, etc., for working men's clubs and socialist societies. But it was the Socialist League under the influence of William Morris that was probably the most potent educational influence during the 1880s. In 1886 a 'Free Education' demonstration was held in Trafalgar Square, immediately followed by a League meeting where it was asserted that the struggle for education 'must be made part of the great stuggle for a complete change in the conditions ot life' – echoing Morris's argument that 'the knowledge we have to help people to is three-fold – to know their own, to know how to take their own and to know how to use their own.'[22] There is little doubt that:

> The earliest English Marxists were extraordinarily able and enthusiastic propagandists. They lectured in Trafalgar Square, at park rostra and on street corners; they published ... newspapers and magazines ... they distributed pamphlets and broadsides and submitted letters to virtually every newspaper in the country. They also contributed articles to the major reviews; they wrote books ... they participated in debates ...

they travelled to Oxford and Cambridge to introduce Marxism to the universities; they campaigned for public office; and they engaged in the translation of Marx's writings. By 1890 Marxism ... was in the forefront of English intellectual life.[23]

In 1899 Ruskin Hall was founded at Oxford 'to educate working men in order to achieve social change'.[24] According to one of its American founders, Walter Vrooman, 'knowledge must be used to emancipate humanity, not to gratify curiosity, blind instincts and desire for respectability'.[25] There was widespread support from the trade unions who saw Ruskin as another source of independent working-class education. By 1907 more than half the total financial contributions for the College were coming from the trade union movement (see 1908 Report, para 9). That same year, the TUC issued an official appeal for support for Ruskin in which it quite bluntly stated 'now that Labour is showing that it is determined to take its rightful position in the country, it more than ever needs the knowledge and training necessary to maintain that position.'[26]

The Ruskin Hall Scheme extended beyond the residential college in Oxford. It also stimulated classes in many parts of the country, particularly in industrial areas. There were 96 such classes in existence by 1902. It also catered for correspondence students, enrolling 1800 during its first two years. Local Ruskin Halls were also established in Manchester, Liverpool, Stockport and Birmingham (although most of these outside activities, except the correspondence courses, were abandoned after 1903, partly because of the emergence of the WEA).

The true independence and socialist commitment of Ruskin might always have been in doubt. Not so the educational activity of the socialist political parties. The SDF organised a number of classes and informal pub discussions to introduce its members to the ideas of Marx and Engels. Its most renowned teacher was John Maclean who by 1906–7 was lecturing to large audiences and conducting classes in various parts of Scotland. Some years later he explained that he wished to see all opportunities for self-development opened up to the working class, but he was 'specially interested in such education as will make revolutionaries ... The very antagonisms in society ... make it ... urgent that the workers should forge their own educational machine for their own class ends.'[27]

The SLP attached great importance to political education: a rigorous and concentrated study of Marxism was essential training for its revolutionary cadres. Sharing the belief of the American SLP leader, Daniel de Leon, that 'a ruling class dominates not only the bodies, but the mind also of the class that it rules', the British SLP 'looked to education to open the workers' eyes to the tricks played by the conjurors of bourgeoisdom, who produced compelling illusions of freedom, plenty and justice out of the realities of poverty, exploitation and arbitrary power. Education, if it was sound, would reveal to the workers the boundless opportunities for human happiness following the overthrow of capitalism.'[28] Workers' interest in education was thus seen as an opportunity for steering them in the direction of socialist revolution. The SLP produced pamphlets advocating the theory and practice of industrial unionism and conducted classes and correspondence courses in Marxism, economics, history, philosophy, logic and literature. These classes played an important part in the development of 'red' Clydeside; and similar classes were organised in other parts of Scotland and also south of the border – for example in Manchester, Newcastle, Reading and London. The classes took place in factories and elsewhere on Sunday afternoons. Class members would then go off to spread their socialist ideas to large audiences who collected at street corners on Sunday evenings.

The syndicalists also recognised the importance of education in propagating their ideas and established a range of educational activities and informal discussion circles. All this independent working-class education had a dramatic effect on Ruskin, where the authorities' attempts to strengthen the College's connections with the University (see below) brought them into conflict with the socialist students, whose SDF, SLP and syndicalist training predisposed them to have nothing to do with the University's bourgeois education. In October 1908 the students founded the Plebs League 'with the avowed aim of providing a platform for pleading the cause of independent working-class education and appealing to the rank and file in the labour movement. Its initial goal was to transform Ruskin College into a genuine *Labour* college run by workers for workers.'[29] This conflict of views as to the real purpose of the College led ultimately to the Ruskin strike in 1909.

This multifarious network of independent education meant that by the early years of the tw 'a fresh generation of young militants was emergii knowledge and prepared to discard the dogmas of (doxy.'[30] It was a frightening prospect for a bourg(liberal values. 'The growth of independent workin the increase of independent working-class actior purveyors of culture bad dreams – red dreams wit plots of dagger and dynamite.'[31]

Into this political dissonance stepped Albert N his proposals for a Workers' Educational Assc conception of education as something ideal in it uncontaminated by the urge for material improv and political change. He believed that access to th of knowledge' in the universities would raise th(such mundane aspirations and 'in spite of the str ful days ... divert the strong movements of the narrow paths of immediate interests.'[32] Mansbri(obvious approval, the criticisms voiced by the (of the Society of Railway Servants of the allege and thoughtless actions of some of his executive (the Taff Vale strike, as an example of the imperat education for those taking an active part in d^m^ such as trade unions. Considering the trade movement's perception of the Taff Vale judgement as blatant class oppression, Mansbridge could hardly have selected a more significant example to demonstrate the real implications of his concept of spiritual, non-materialist education for the working class. If Mansbridge was naively unconscious of the political implications of his approach, this was not true of many of the WEA's influential supporters, such as Dr John Percival, Bishop of Hereford, who advised the Chairman of the Oxford Delegacy in 1906 that 'to exercise its highest influence among the working class generally', Oxford should work through the leading trade unions.[33] The

WEA was welcomed as a golden opportunity to exercise this influence:

> Mansbridge's view of education, echoing so completely their own ideas, was totally acceptable to the Oxford liberals. The new Association promised to be a safe beneficiary of their liberalism, an ideal opportunity for acquiring a veneer of working-class participation and support without risking any fundamental upheavals ... Similarly, the Government (or at least its Board of Education) was seeking ways of fending off accusations of being 'permeated with a caste feeling ... and ... entirely estranged from working class needs.' It attempted to do so by appointing D.J. Shackleton, a Labour M.P., and Mansbridge to the Consultative Committee of the Board of Education and also, at the 1907 Oxford Conference, making the famous offer of a share of the 'golden stream' ... Support for the WEA was seen as a sound political investment against extremism.[34]

In fact, support for the WEA was part of the liberal social and welfare reformism with which the new Liberal Government after 1906 hoped to placate and incorporate the labour movement. It was part of a well established strategy to contain and subordinate working-class politics. 'Increasingly between 1890 and 1914 the attempt was made to defuse unrest by incorporating labour representatives within limited bargaining institutions and by the development of state-sponsored social welfare policies'.[35] While the Conservatives were not averse to this strategy, they were more inclined to confront the labour movement in a head-on counter-attack. It was 'New Liberalism' which aimed to contain the socialist impulses and head off revolutionism by offering 'limited socialism' as a political alternative to the Marxian socialism:

> From the 1890s onwards, New Liberalism had a profound impact on working-class politics, helping to persuade working-class activists, even while they agitated for an independent Party and, many of them, looked to socialism as an ultimate goal, that their interests lay in co-operation with the new breed of liberal in a drive to abolish poverty via the legislative intervention of the state ... Whatever its ameliorative

effects early twentieth-century social reform embodied a counter-attack on democratic and working-class institutions at least as formidable as the employers' attack on trade unions in the 1890s.[36]

The Liberals' social welfare policy after 1906 was intended both to increase industrial efficiency and introduce mechanisms for disciplining labour as well as providing a minimal social safety net. The government grants towards the relief of the unemployed, the old age pensions, and Beveridge's new labour exchanges, all introduced between 1906–9, involved labour in a partnership with the state. This was even more true of the National Insurance Act (1911) which provided a national system of insurance for sickness and unemployment and included the trade unions amongst the 'approved societies' empowered to administer this insurance scheme. The trade unions thus became a part of the state machinery. A history of the small National Union of Boot and Shoe Operatives shows how its members held 100 positions on statutory bodies and committees by 1912. 'There were now members of Old-Age Pension Committees, members of National Insurance Act Advisory Committees, a member of a Water Board and School Managers. All these changes meant that the union was ... becoming more closely knit both with society and with the state ... It was co-operating with state machinery to administer new and complicated social legislation'.[37] The labour movement's involvement in this welfare statism was an involvement in social control. This was well understood by Liberal experts and particularly Lloyd George 'who by 1912 regarded the parliamentary socialists as "the best policemen for the Syndicalists"'.[38] State aid for adult education was another, if small, part of this welfare state control. Following the publication of the 1908 Report, this consisted very largely of grant-aid for tutorial classes.

After five rather frustrating years trying to adapt University Extension to its own purpose, the WEA called a conference in Oxford in 1907 to approve the formation of the committee which produced the 1908 Report. One of the main objectives of the Report was to secure University control of the education of the leading members of the working class in order 'to guide their general outlook ... towards social harmony.'[39] From the middle of the nineteenth century there had been a growing awareness amongst the more liberal elements at Oxford and Cambridge, headed by T.H. Green, of the need to foment social harmony by exalting citizenship of an overarching corporate state above all material values, thereby preventing the workers, understandably angered by undeniable injustices, from 'destroying, in their fury, not only unfairness and exploitation, but also civilization itself.'[40] This social harmony was made manifest at a meeting in Mansbridge's lodgings in Wellington Square on the evening of the 1907 Oxford Conference, idyllically described by Alfred Zimmern, a member of the Oxford radical reform Catiline Club and of the WEA:

> The Bishop and a number of workmen were staying in the house and they were joined by one friend after another who dropped in, in Oxford fashion, for a talk. Most branches of education were repre-sented: Whitehall (which sat on the window-sill), Cambridge, in the person of a Fellow of Trinity, the Oxford Professoriate and the elemen-tary teacher; there was capital in the shape of a London banker and there was labour galore (in both sexes) and a Bishop to complete the picture. Wellington Square is not perhaps the place a romance-writer would select for his vision of Utopia; but that night at least it seemed a 'centre of the intellectual aspirations of the whole community'.[41]

The Report itself regretted the growing tendency towards class divisions in society which made it 'increasingly difficult for the various sections of the community to appreciate each other's circumstances and aspirations' (in the manner of the Wellington Square evening) and *'for this reason* it seems important that the leaders of every class should have an opportunity of obtaining a wide outlook on the historical development and economic condi-tion of the whole English community, such as is given by a University education' (para 78, writer's italics). Such an education, the outward mark of which was 'a broad reasoned view of things and a sane measure of social values', would equip the workmen with 'the civic qualities which enable him to co-operate with his fellows and to judge wisely on matters which concern not only himself, but the whole country to which he belongs' (para 82). 'By broadening his knowledge and strengthening his judgement', this Oxford education 'would make him at once a more efficient servant of his own society and a *more potent influence on the side of industrial peace*' (para 139, writer's italics). In this way, the working-class students' education was envisaged as 'a means, not only of developing their own powers of enjoyment, but of enabling them to exercise an influence for good in the social life of the factory and town' (para137). Thus was social harmony the very antithesis of class struggle – an unquestioned doctrine of the workers' education advocated by the Report. On this vital point there was no common ground with the independent working-class education movement whose object was summarised by the Plebs League mandate: 'Nothing more nor less than the education of the workers in the interests of the workers'.[42]

There was a little more agreement over the need for the working class to organise and control its own education. The Report recommended that a representative body of workpeople should be largely responsible for organising and promoting the classes and should 'have a voice in selecting the teacher ...', although this was somewhat diluted in the summary of recommendations (para 89 and Recommendation IV). By giving the representative body a 'controlling voice in the selection of a teacher' it was hoped to avoid the imposition of teachers who had 'an unconscious class bias' (para 90). It was felt that the selected teachers should not only have the neccessary qualifications, but should also have a knowledge of and sympathy with working-class life, habits of thought and points of view (paras 100–02). But there were to be strict limits to this consumer control. It was not intended to imply that 'Oxford should, "tune her pulpits" to meet the view of any class' (para 90) – echoing the fears already expressed by Hudson Shaw and J.A.R. Marriott and later to be expressed by other critics.[43] Control of the *content* of education was to remain firmly in the hands of the University. 'While the management and organisation of the class shall be mainly in the hands of workpeople, the selection of curricula and guidance in reading must be the duty of the University acting in co-operation with workpeople' (para 92). This was a far cry from independent working-class education, as the first editorial of *Plebs* was quick to point out:

If the education of the workers is to square with the ultimate object of the workers – social emancipation, then it is neccessary that the control of such an educational institution must be in the hands of the workers ... Beware of the sounding brass and the tinkling cymbal of ruling class professed sympathies with labour.[44]

In the same way that New Liberalism aimed to incorporate the working class within the welfare state, so the Report envisaged working-class incorporation within the educational system, to minimise the attraction of a dangerous alternative system. Therefore working-class representation on the body organising and promoting the classes and on some of the governing bodies of the University was advocated because such representatives might make a useful contribution, because it would give them a valuable insight into the working of university institutions and because 'it secures the confidence and co-operation of large bodies of men who might otherwise be inclined to distrust Oxford' (para 85). Even more significantly, the Report's Recommendation V, that Ruskin students should be awarded one-year certificates and two-year diplomas, effectively incorporated the College more closely within the University – precisely what the Ruskin students, fired with enthusiasm for independent working-class education, were attempting to avoid. The Report clearly intended 'to change Ruskin from a labour college into a college preparatory to university studies, involving a transformation of its whole ethos and purpose.'[45] Lord Curzon, Chancellor of the University, quite explicitly referred to subjecting Ruskin to the University's influences and discipline – to prevent its being dominated by the narrow views of particular political or economic schools or recruiting solely from one party.[46]

Another important premise of the Report was that working-class students should not be educated to abandon their class, or escape from it but 'should remain in it and raise its whole level' by becoming leaders in their trade unions, or in their workshops, or by becoming working-class representatives on public bodies (para 81). Their education would 'enable workmen to fulfil with greater efficiency the duties which they owe to their own class and ... to the whole nation' by becoming full-time officials in trade unions, trade councils, friendly societies, co-operative societies, etc; by representing Labour in the House of Commons, in local government and on public bodies; and by becoming teachers of the tutorial classes – to help other working-class students (paras137–42). Thus, '... with minds enlarged by impartial study they ... may become the future teachers and leaders, the philosophers and economists, of the working classes' (para 144).

But what was this impartial study that formed the basis of the Report's grand educational vision: the promised land? The Plebs League certainly had no faith in it:

> No working-class student can undergo a University education and come through it untainted ... University life is the breeding ground of reaction. It incites by its very nature towards breaking away from working-class aspirations ... [Oxford University] is the place where men are taught to govern, it is the governing class who control it, it is they who decide what shall be taught and how it shall be taught and as the interests of these people are in direct antagonism to the interest of the workers, it is sheer folly for the latter to think that any good can come of sending any of their number there.[47]

The notion of impartiality or political neutrality had already been used by the organisers of the 1907 Oxford Conference to exclude association with the educational programme of the TUC from the agenda.[48] This provides some indication of how all-embracing their impartiality really was, but the real test was to be found in the content of the education provided. This is why the University's determination to retain control over the content and curricula was so crucial. A key issue was the nature of the economics classes, especially 'whether Marxist economics should be taught or merely ignored or refuted.'[49] Appendix VII of the Report offered some model courses of study 'to indicate upon what general lines the class teaching would proceed', including a course in economics. This was based very heavily on Marshall's *Economics of Industry* (described as 'undoubtedly the most authorative and sympathetic' textbook, and a variety of other Liberal and Fabian writers. The proposed syllabus did allow that 'if many members of the class have socialistic views' part of Marx's *Capital* or Hyndman's *Economics of Socialism* should be used. However, this constituted a very small part of the total course, apparently included as a sop to the socialistic students, to be omitted altogether for non-socialists! Moreover, 'the teacher who adopts this course must ... be very sure that the criticism of Marx, implicit in the ordinary textbook, is equally carefully explained' – a warning not applied to any other parts of the course or text. It would be difficult to be more partial than that.

The history and political science courses, as was to be expected, laid a heavy emphasis on constitutionalism. The modern world course did include an option on the working-class movement in Europe and England (which aroused some opposition at Oxford)[50] and there was an option in the recent English history course on the labour-socialist movement since 1880. This did refer to the influence of Marx, Hyndman and Henry George, but was predominantly Fabian in its approach, as were the majority of the history and politics courses. For example, trade unions and the co-operative movement were excluded from the working-class political organisations covered in one of the recent English history options – they were studied separately as *non-political* organisations. This typifies the Liberal/Fabian influence which pervaded most of the syllabuses.

The 'impartial' study of historical and economic questions fostered by the tutorial classes from 1908 onwards 'was something very different from the Marxist studies promoted by [the] socialist groups which had inherited the earlier Socialist League slogan: 'educate – agitate – organise'.[51] This approach saw education as leading directly on to political action. From this perspective the 1908 Report was seen as an attempt by Oxford to surcharge the brains of working-class leaders 'with the ideas of a class above them, so that their interests may become identical with the interests of that class' and the WEA was regarded as 'hopelessly entangled in the class interests of those whose body and blood it is: ... a graft which only appears when the movement of the workers begins to gain in power.'[52]

After 1908, 'the idea of a separate working-class educational system began to fade'[53] (at least in part owing to the effectiveness of *Oxford and Working Class Education*), and the WEA and the tutorial class movement grew from strength to strength. These provided an education that was 'broadly liberal, sometimes radical, sometimes pluralist, but essentially orthodox and anti-Marxist in its overall tenor',[54] for the working class and in particular for the emerging leaders of the labour movement. 'Its comfortable affinity with the British liberal tradition seemed to offer a welcome alternative to the revolutionary perspective of the Communist Party and the National Council of Labour Colleges – the perceived real enemies of the State. For all its occasional lapses, [this] adult education movement was welcomed by the establishment as a bulwark against revolutionism, a moderating influence and a form of social control. It helped to channel and reduce pressures and conflict, neutralise class antagonism and integrate the working class into British society – just like its "partner", the Labour Party'.[55] Its value as an antidote to class struggle was readily acknowledged by a Conservative President of the Board of Education some seventeen years after the publication of *Oxford and Working Class Education*:

> In adult education there is a continual struggle going on between the Universities and those bodies, like the Workers' Educational Association, who work with the Universities, on the one hand, and the Communist or semi-Communist Labour Colleges on the other. Hitherto the Workers' Educational Association and the University Extension people have been able to make headway against these undesirable propagandists because, largely owing to Government assistance, they can offer better facilities. On the whole too, I think the education that they do offer is extraordinarily useful ... If we force the WEA and the Universities to cut down their work we shall not choke off the demand for local classes which is extraordinarily strong in all parts of the country, but we shall open a wide door to the Labour Colleges and I believe that the result will be deplorable. In fact my own view is that £100,000 spent annually on this kind of work, properly controlled, would be about the best police expenditure we could indulge in.[56]

This article appears courtesy of Nottingham University Continuing Education Press. It originally appeared in Oxford and Working-Class Education: A New Introduction to the 1908

Report, *Sylvia Harrop (ed)*, Continuing Education Press, University of Nottingham 1987.

REFERENCES

1. Quoted in J.F. and Winifred Horrabin, *Working Class Education*, The Labour Publishing Co., 1924, p29.
2. T. Lane, *The Union Makes Us Strong*, Arrow Books, 1974, p88.
3. E. Hobsbawm, *Labouring Men*, Weidenfeld & Nicolson, 1968, p325.
4. See, eg., J. Hinton, *Labour and Socialism: A History of the British Labour Movement 1867-1974*, Brighton, Wheatsheaf, 1983, pp40-63.
5. Hobsbawm, *Labouring Men*, p231.
6. P. Adelman, *The Rise of the Labour Party 1880-1945*, Longman, 1972, p7.
7. Hinton, *Labour and Socialism*, p51.
8. K. Marx and F. Engels, *On Britain*, Moscow, 1953, p523.
9. Adelman, *The Rise of the Labour Party*, p16.
10. Hinton, *Labour and Socialism*, p68.
11. *Ibid*, p75.
12. W. Kendall, *The Revolutionay Movement in Britain 1900-21*, Weidenfeld & Nicolson, 1969, p.7.
13. R. Challinor, *The Origins of British Bolshevism*, Croom Helm 1977, p281.
14. *Ibid* p53.
15. B. Holton, *British Syndicalism 1900-1914*, Pluto Press, 1976, p39.
16. Challinor, *Origins of British Bolshevism*, p97.
17. Kendall, *The Revolutionay Movement in Britain*, p22.
18. Anne Phillips and T. Putman, 'Education for Emancipation: the Movement for Independent Working Class Education 1902-1928', *Capital and Class*, No. 10, 1980, pp18-42 (p20).
19. S. Macintyre, *A Proletarian Science*, Cambridge University Press, 1980, p71. See also J.F.C. Harrison, 'Underground Education in the Nineteenth Century', *Eighth Mansbridge Memorial Lecture*, Leeds University 1971; and J. Rée, *Proletarian Philosophers*, Clarendon Press, Oxford 1984, pp6-14.
20. B. Simon, *Education and the Labour Movement 1870-1920*, Lawrence & Wishart 1965, pp303 and 313.
21. Horrabin, *Working Class Education*, p40.
22. *Ibid.*, pp42 and 73.
23. K. Willis, 'The Introduction and Critical Reception of Marxist Thought in Britain 1850-1900', *Historical Journal*, Vol. 20, No. 2, 1977, pp417-59

(p438). However, Willis goes on to show that Marxism did not penetrate very far, or greatly influence English political thought.

24. H. Pollins, *The History of Ruskin College*, Ruskin College Library, 1984, p9.
25. *Ibid.*, p10.
26. Quoted in Horrabin, *Working Class Education*, p33 and Simon, *Education and the Labour Movement*, p.319.
27. Quoted in J. H. Roberts, 'The National Council of Labour Colleges: An Experiment in Workers' Education', M.Sc. thesis, University of Edinburgh, 1970, p45.
28. Rée, *Proletarian Philosophers*, p13.
29. J.P.M. Millar, *The Labour College Movement*, NCLC Publishing Society, 1979, p7.
30. Challinor, *The Origins of British Bolshevism*, p115.
31. Editorial in *Plebs*, Vol. 1, No. 2, March 1909, p22.
32. A. Mansbridge, 'A Plan of Action', *University Extension Journal*, March 1903, reprinted in A. Mansbridge, *The Kingdom of the Mind*, 2nd edn. Manchester Meridan Press, 1946, p6.
33. Quoted in J.S. Marriott, 'Oxford and working-class adult education: A foundation myth re-examined', *History of Education*, Vol. 12, No. 4, 1983 pp285-99 (p291).
34. R. Fieldhouse, *The Workers' Educational Association: Aims and Achievements 1903-1977*, Syracuse University, New York 1977, pp7-8.
35. Holton, *British Syndicalism*, p31.
36. Hinton, *Labour and Socialism*, pp38 and 76.
37. A. Fox, *A History of the National Union of Boot and Shoe Operators*, Blackwell, Oxford 1958, pp329-30.
38. Holton, *British Syndicalism*, p36, quoting a speech by Lloyd George on 19 March 1912.
39. Simon, *Education and the Labour Movement*, pp314-5.
40. Rée, *Proletarian Philosophers*, pp15-17.
41. A.E.Z., 'The Workers at the Oxford Summer Meeting', *The Oxford Magazine*, 24 October 1907.
42. Editorial in *Plebs*, Vol. 1, No. 1, Feb. 1909, p4.
43. B. Jennings, 'The Oxford Report Reconsidered', *Studies in Adult Education*, Vol. 7, No. 1, 1975, pp53-65 (pp58, 60 and 62).
44. *Plebs*, Vol. 1, No. 1, p3.
45. Simon, *Education and the Labour Movement*, p.318. See also Pollins, *History of Ruskin College*, pp20 and 23-5.
46. Lord Curzon, *Principles and Methods of University Reform*, 1909, pp63-4.
47. Editorial in *Plebs*, Vol. 1, No. 3, April 1909, p44.

48. Jennings, 'The Oxford Report Reconsidered', p57.
49. Simon, *Education and the Labour Movement*, p321. This referred to Ruskin, but applied equally to the tutorial classes.
50. J.B. Rye, 'Oxford and the Working Class', *The Nineteenth Century*, Vol. 65, pp521-34, quoted in Jennings, 'The Oxford Report Reconsidered', p62.
51. Simon, *Education and the Labour Movement*, p311.
52. Editorial in *Plebs*, Vol. 1, No. 2 (March 1909), pp22-3.
53. Rée, *Proletarian Philosophers*, p20. See also Phillips and Putnam, 'Education for Emancipation', *passim*.
54. R. Fieldhouse, 'The Ideology of Responsible Body Adult Education Teaching 1925-1950', *Studies in Adult Education*, Vol. 15, 1983, pp11-35 (p.28).
55. R. Fieldhouse, 'Conformity and Conflict in English Responsible Body Adult Education 1925-1950', *Studies in the Education of Adults*, Vol. 17 No. 2, 1985.
56. Public Record Office, T.161/186/S.17166, Lord Eustace Percy to Walter Guinness, 7 Oct. 1925.

'Long-haired intellectuals and busybodies': Ruskin, student radicalism, and civil rights in Northern Ireland

BOB PURDIE

STUDENT POWER

In the late 1960s Oxford was a radical city and because of its special status amongst English cities student protest got a great deal of international publicity. As an ancient seat of learning it had geological layers of ritual and regulation, but it also had a significant working-class population. For the revolutionary left of the time Oxford offered a prime opportunity to implement the 'red bases' strategy which saw 'student power' as a force which could generate a wider revolutionary upsurge, on the model of the May-June events of 1968 in Paris.

1968 was a dramatic year in the city. The spirit of the times was reflected in slogans which appeared on the walls of Balliol College; 'Positivism Out! Dialectics In!' and 'Aphorism is the Death Rattle of Revolution'.[1] For the first time a significant number of undergraduates became involved in direct action. There were major student demonstrations against the Proctors (the University officials in charge of student discipline); against racism; and against right-wing politicians. There was a rally to commemorate Jan Palach, the Prague student who burned himself to death in protest at the Soviet invasion of Czechoslovakia. The city mourned the assassinated Martin Luther King and it repudiated Enoch Powell, opposing the racism stirred up by his statements on immigration. Ruskin students were involved in all these events.

They were not, however, typical Oxford students. They were older and they often had a background in militant trade unionism, or left-wing socialism, or both. In a city historically split between university and non-university residents, they were neither town nor gown. And the 'red base' strategy was less relevant for them because it depended on a confrontation with sclerotic bureaucratic institutions used to treating students as schoolchildren. The College staff and Executive responded quickly to demands for change, thus diffusing potential protest action. There was a revolt against the College's attachment to the Oxford University Special Diplomas, which all students sat and which subordinated the College to a very traditional academic curriculum. Two members of the teaching staff, Raphael Samuel and David Selbourne, took the lead in pressing for change. In a document of May 1968 the former wrote:

> Ruskin ought to be run, so far as is possible, as a socialist college – that is experienced as a co-operative effort on the part of students, tutors and staff. As a college of Adult Education, recruited largely from the Labour Movement, we ought to be able to conduct our college life in a distinctive way, one which reflects the maturity of our students and the values for which we stand. This is very far from the case at present. We have, in fact, very little control over the environment in which we work; it is decided from outside by the omnipresent demands of the [Special] Diploma which dictates ... everything we do.

A joint consultative committee was set up to consider student participation. By the end of the year the pragmatic Victor Treadwell had produced proposals for student representation which channelled 'student power' into a set of committee structures which kept student activists tied up in meetings. The creation of new, internally examined, diplomas ended reliance on the University Special Diplomas. The College had contained the rebellion by routinising it.

A BOURGEOIS UNIVERSITY

Radical action by Ruskin students was also directed beyond the College itself. In April 1968 Enoch Powell made his notorious speech on Commonwealth immigration. Ruskin students attended an emergency meeting of the University Labour Club and reported that some black workers at the Cowley car factory had found racist leaflets in their lockers. Left-wing undergraduates responded with a rally and leaflets at the factory gates. But in doing so they had broken a statute of the University which required permission for political activity from the Proctors.

Ninety undergraduates signed a letter to the Proctors announcing where and when they would break the statute and proceeded to leaflet the factory about a new productivity scheme. The undergraduates were called before the Proctors who announced that they were to be let off without a fine because they had 'admitted the offence'.[2] In June a 'Committee of 90' was set up to campaign for the right of students to take part in political activity. The Committee gave the Proctors an 'ultimatum' to lift all restrictions, and a militant demonstration of up to 200 students gathered outside their meeting in the Clarendon Building. More than a hundred protesters forced their way through the doors, where they spent two hours arguing with the Proctors. Eventually the authorities gave way and relinquished the right to veto student political activities.

An Oxford Revolutionary Socialist Students Society (ORSS) was set up following these events. In October they picketed the Sheldonian Theatre, to protest against the University matriculation ceremonies which, according to the *Oxford Mail*, they denounced as a 'ludicrous and expensive ceremony of initiation into a bourgeois university ...'.[3] The *Mail* also reported that Ben Cosin of Nuffield College spoke from a step ladder, declaring that 'only socialism would destroy the division between the university and society. A don came out of the Bodleian and said, "Ben, some of us are trying to read books up there. You are making an awful lot of noise"'.[4]

Later that month ORSS supporters burst into the Randolph Hotel and broke up a meeting of the Society for Individual

Freedom, a far right group. When they heckled the Conservative MP Sir Cyril Osborne in Regents Park College in November he told them, 'Boy, I'd like to have had you on the parade ground'.[5] On 5 November the ORSS tried to storm a meeting of Congregation, the University's ruling body, demanding to be let in to address the meeting. The doors were blocked and they clashed with University staff. Six students were summoned to appear before the Proctors later that month, but a human wall of 250 students blocked their way. However a couple of days later the Proctors outwitted the ORSS by letting fifty of them occupy the Clarendon Building while the disciplinary hearing actually took place in the Examination Schools.

Ruskin involvement caused some problems for relations between the College and the University. In January 1969 Billy Hughes, the Principal, reported to the College Executive Committee on a meeting with the Proctors to discuss 'problems which might arise if members of Ruskin participate in actions directed against the University'. They had agreed that he would use his influence to restrain them from disrupting University activities, and he had issued a statement to students:

> ... if the College received privileges from the University we incurred obligations in return ... Ruskin students taking part in activities against the University could not expect immunity from the consequences. I made it clear that there was no question of victimisation for political activities and that no threats of any kind had been made, and asked for co-operation, restraint and commonsense.[6]

Stephen Kelly, a Ruskin student at that time, remembered that this made Ruskin students even more determined to participate in the biggest student protest of the time. It followed the discovery in February 1969, by students occupying the Registry at Warwick University, of files on student radicals. A demonstration of four hundred took place outside the Clarendon Building demanding the right to see Oxford University's files. Stephen Kelly recalled that they were unable to get past the gates until some hefty Ruskin students pushed their way to the front and shoved. The gates snapped open and thirty students surged in to occupy the building.[7] In a second occupation several hundred participated. The occupation lasted nearly a week and at its peak 2000 turned out to demonstrate in support.

However, the protest petered out amidst disagreements over strategy. The ORSS got a good deal of publicity and provoked even more exasperation, but it was more sound than fury and it was tiny in comparison to Oxford's student body of 10,300. Its demonstrations typically attracted a couple of hundred and it failed to break out of its own narrow circle of activists. The Proctors might have helped by dealing out heavy handed punishments; but they responded to student protest fairly moderately.

THE COLOUR OF BROTHERHOOD

Ruskin students had catalysed this wave of protest by their intervention in the Labour Club. But they could not take a full part because they were not subject to the Proctors and the University regulations. This made issues on which they could work with both town and gown important. One issue was the war in Vietnam, and the ORSS organised five coaches to the Vietnam solidarity demonstration in London on 27 October. The most important issue was racism. The upsurge of militancy by black people in the United States; the unleashing of right wing and racist groups in Britain by Enoch Powell's speeches on immigration; the white settler rebellion in Rhodesia and the running sore of apartheid in South Africa. These offered a focus for a wide range of left-wing and liberal groups. The high level of interest in Oxford was shown in October 1967 when the British Black Power leader, Michael X spoke to a meeting in Brasenose College. Over 200 turned up to hear him and the meeting had to be moved at short notice to the dining hall of nearby All Souls College.

In May 1968 Christ Church Cathedral was packed to commemorate the recently assassinated Martin Luther King. The preacher was the Reverend Kenneth Leech, a prominent Christian Socialist known for his work in London. His sermon caught the mood of the times:

Red in theological as well as political mythology is the colour of brother-hood, of the blood which unites mankind in solidarity, and to Christians the blood red banner of the Son of Man is the banner of justice and freedom. But red too is the blood of the martyrs, and we come together to remember one, Martin Luther King. We celebrate his living and dying with gratitude and joy, and yet with apprehension. There is a cynical irony in the fact that so soon after the American Freedom fighters marched for Martin Luther King a section of British dockers should march for Enoch Powell with placards saying 'Back Britain not Black Britain'.[8]

Ruskin students responded to Powell's speech by calling a one day strike against racism on 1 May which was supported by the College and the staff. There was a lecture and entertainment in the College in the afternoon and a march through Oxford in the early evening. This attracted about 2000 participants and Billy Hughes marched at its head. On 8 June there was a 'teach-in' on racism, which took over the College for a series of speeches and discussions. On 20 January 1969 there was a demonstration against Enoch Powell who was speaking to a Conservative meeting in the Town Hall. A number of Ruskin students were arrested and the students set up a defence fund to pay their fines.

The College Executive Committee made it clear that it was not appropriate for college funds to be used for the fines, but they were keen to support moderate student opposition to racism. They initiated a fund to offer scholarships to immigrant workers and supported various anti-racist educational initiatives. In an attempt to secure his early release, they offered a staff position to a former Ruskin student Dave Kitson, who had been imprisoned in South Africa for his involvement in Umkhonto we Sizwe, the military wing of the African National Congress. The students organised a Kitson Committee to demand his freedom and to support his family. The Committee organised a march from Oxford to London over the Whit weekend 21-25 May 1968, and it continued for many years to campaign against racism and fascism.

Towards the end of May 1968 the Oxford Committee for Racial Integration (OCRI) drew attention to racial discrimination by a women's hairdresser in the Cowley Road called 'Annette'. Two young black women, students from the Oxford College of Further Education, had been refused appointments. They were allegedly told, 'we do not want your nationality here'.[9] There was a small picket outside the shop one Saturday afternoon. But students from the ORSS, Ruskin College and the College of FE adopted a more militant approach.

In the mid-1960s the desegregation campaigns in the United States had developed the tactic of the 'sit-in'. When a black person had been refused service in a shop or restaurant, demonstrators occupied the premises and refused to move until the discrimination was ended. The Oxford students adopted similar tactics. They returned to the salon the week after the picket with larger numbers. Eight demonstrators went into the shop on a signal from a young South African woman who had been refused service. Others sat down on the pavement outside, blocking access to the premises. Another group of supporters stood on the opposite pavement.

The protesters were assaulted by the proprietor and her husband. The police ignored this but arrested 39 demonstrators. When 37 of them came up in court the following June they were fined a token sum of £1.00 each. No less than fourteen were from Ruskin; by far the largest group from any college. One of those fined was David Selbourne. He told the *Oxford Times*, 'As a tutor in a multi-racial college I consider it my profound obligation to play my part in preventing discrimination against my fellow students because of the colour of their skin.'[10] Bernard Reaney, one of the arrested Ruskin students, remembered:

> We planned that every one of us accused would make a long speech denouncing Annette's and racism in general. But the magistrates abandoned the proceedings after one or two speeches as I remember, and fined us a derisory £1 (never paid as far as I know). The public gallery was packed with noisy supporters and the magistrates were successfully intimidated. We sang the Red Flag inside the court and marched out to be met by a huge crowd outside the court as well.[11]

In July, following another mass picket and more arrests, the proprietor conceded defeat and gave an undertaking not to discriminate. She claimed not to have operated a 'colour bar' but to have lacked the equipment and skills needed to deal with 'frizzy' hair. The OCRI ended the campaign, satisfied that their demands had been met.

Another obvious issue for Ruskin student involvement would have been unrest in the car factory and there were a number of key disputes around this time. Some leading shop stewards at Cowley were left-wing radicals and shared the concerns of students for issues like racism and the Vietnam war. Like them they were inspired by the May-June events in Paris, and the general strike and wave of factory occupations which followed the outbreak of student militancy. But no effective links were formed; the biggest obstacle was the difficulty of students, even Ruskin students, seeking to influence factory workers from the outside.[12]

COME TO NORTHERN IRELAND AND LOSE YOUR VOTE!

On 5 October 1968 television news all over the world showed a police attack on a Northern Ireland Civil Rights Association (NICRA) demonstration in the Northern Ireland city of Derry (officially called 'Londonderry'). The Vietnam protests in London had resulted in clashes, but the police there were more circumspect and restrained. In Derry demonstrators, including Gerry Fitt, the Republican Labour Party MP for West Belfast, were seen being batoned without apparent provocation. Water cannon, not used in Britain, sprayed people indiscriminately and rioting broke out and continued until the following evening.

Civil rights and opposition to discrimination against a minority group had become an explosive political issue within a part of the United Kingdom previously considered a political backwater. One consequence within Northern Ireland was the creation of a student organisation, the Peoples Democracy, which campaigned for civil rights and appealed to students in Britain for support.

Irish people all over the English-speaking world responded to the Derry events by organising support for the civil rights movement in Northern Ireland; and in many places an alliance was formed with the youthful new left. Mass meetings were held and large amounts of money were raised, but these solidarity campaigns had significant internal tensions and soon broke up in internal disputes. They were often more trouble than help to the civil rights movement in Northern Ireland.[13]

Ruskin students also responded. An 'Oxford Committee for Democracy in Northern Ireland' was set up by a Ruskin student, Gerry Doyle. He told the *Oxford Mail* that its objectives were 'to secure a One Man One Vote system in Northern Ireland and to eliminate discrimination in housing'. The committee of eight was described as 'non-political and non-sectarian'.[14] This was one of the earliest groups (possibly the very first) formed specifically to support the Northern Ireland civil rights movement. It coincided with the setting up of the Peoples Democracy in Belfast.

Like many British cities Oxford had a vigorous Irish community. They joined with student radicals in setting up the 'Northern Ireland Civil Rights Oxford Committee' (NICROC) which soon merged with the Oxford Committee for Democracy in Northern Ireland. NICROC issued a leaflet headed 'Have You Thought About Your Country Lately?' It went on:

Where in the United Kingdom
- Can money get you a vote?
- Can you be jailed indefinitely without trial?
- Must you state your religion to get a job?
- Do the police carry guns?
- Are there white British ghettos?

Come to Northern Ireland and lose your vote!

These points reflected the grievances which had led to the civil rights movement in Northern Ireland. At that time there was a property franchise for local government which allowed plural voting for owners of businesses, but denied the vote to non-householders. The Special Powers Act, passed in the 1920s to deal with serious IRA insurgency, was still on the statute book, (although it had not actually been used since the end of the last IRA campaign in 1962).

Many private and local government employers operated blatant or covert discriminatory recruitment policies, which disadvantaged more Catholics than Protestants. The Royal Ulster Constabulary, an overwhelmingly Protestant force, normally wore side-arms. The 'B' Special Constabulary was an armed Protestant militia, feared and resented by Catholics. There was residential segregation in many areas of Northern Ireland. Although a great deal of the segregation was voluntary, it exacerbated a severe housing shortage which disproportionately affected Catholics.

The Northern Ireland civil rights movement began in the mid-1960s when opponents of the Unionist government adopted the tactics and some of the rhetoric of the black civil rights movement in the USA. 'Civil rights' was a new way of thinking about an old problem. Voting rights, constituency boundaries, and the discriminatory allocation of housing and jobs were longstanding grievances for Catholics. By the 1960s the potential for grievance had become much greater because public employment had grown in size and public provision of services, particularly of housing, was much more significant. The structure of local government allowed quite blatant discrimination, particularly where councils were too small to develop bureaucratic procedures. In some of these councils the allocation of particular jobs or council houses was decided by vote in a council chamber divided into bitter Unionist and Nationalist factions.

Hitherto the political response of most Catholics had been to demand a united Ireland, in which the Unionists would be deprived of power. But a new generation of educated Catholics was dissatisfied with this strategy, which they perceived as sterile and sectarian. At the same time increasing numbers of enlightened Protestants were criticising the sectarian basis of the society.

The Northern Ireland civil rights movement was innovatory in three significant ways. First, it demanded for the nationalist minority the rights enjoyed by all other British citizens. Second, it dissociated the discrimination issue from the aspiration to end partition. And third, it demanded rights for *everyone* in Northern Ireland, not just for Catholics. Poor Protestants shared the disadvantages created by plural voting and a property franchise for local government elections. The movement hoped to enlist their support, as well as that of liberal and progressive middle-class Protestants.

This support did not materialise to any significant extent. Instead the civil rights movement alienated most Protestants through street demonstrations. As I explained in my book on the origins of the civil rights movement, *Politics in the Streets*, street marches were the most inappropriate form of political action the civil rights movement could have adopted.[15] In Northern Ireland marches were seen as a sectarian claim on territory. The movement ended up on the streets, however, because other means of exerting pressure had not worked. The Northern Ireland Government would not listen; the courts were closed because legal aid was not available. What caused the greatest frustration was the fact that the Westminster government and parliament would not respond effectively.

Discrimination was not as intense nor as widespread as anti-Unionist propaganda suggested. Catholics did control local government in places where they had a sufficiently large majority to make gerrymandering impossible. They were not excluded from the judicial bench. They were admitted to the police force and the civil service. But there were barriers against their full participation in the state. Local government electoral boundaries were arranged in some places so as to give a Unionist minority a majority of seats on local councils. The bench and police force required an oath of loyalty to the Crown which many nationalists could not, in conscience, take. There were informal, but real, barriers against Catholic promotion beyond a certain point in the civil service. Unionist refusal to concede that discrimination existed led many Catholics to believe that it was a deliberate policy. And the rhetoric of Unionist leaders, including Prime Ministers, was often such as to reinforce the alienation and sense of exclusion felt by most Catholics.

The first public activity organised by NICROC was a demonstration held in Oxford on Saturday 30 November 1968. The march was led by three Irish pipers (who recognised that it was St Andrew's Day by playing 'A Scottish Soldier' in addition to 'The Wearing of the Green'.) In the front rank was the main speaker, Gerry Fitt MP. The 250 marchers made their way from the Plain, on the far side of Magdalen Bridge, to Ruskin College in Walton Street, a route which took them through the main shopping thoroughfares of High Street and Cornmarket. They carried placards which read: 'One Man One Vote' and chanted slogans. Some were reported to have chanted the Vietnam Solidarity Campaign slogan, 'Ho, Ho, Ho Chi Minh'.

The march culminated in a rally in Buxton Hall in Ruskin College. Gerry Fitt made a plea for the British Prime Minster, Harold Wilson, to intervene and warned 'Unless civil rights are given to the people of Ulster the only alternative will be civil war'.

> The situation is fraught with danger. Unless it is brought to an early conclusion it could lead to serious loss of life. I hope no-one will be killed in the months and years ahead and I call upon the working people of Britain to help us in our demands for civil rights in Northern Ireland.

He recalled a statement of Wilson's at the Labour Party conference that Labour was a party of human rights, and said: 'I ask the British Prime Minister from this building tonight to apply that philosophy to my people in Northern Ireland'.[16]

Fitt's speech reflected the deteriorating situation in Northern Ireland. Civil rights activities and loyalist counter-demonstrations were contributing to serious sectarian polarisation. In the United States the civil rights movement was able to maintain a non-violent strategy, but in Northern Ireland civil rights leaders were finding it more and more difficult to hold the line against rioting and retaliatory violence from the Catholic community. Many older people had memories of civil strife from the 1930s and feared the consequences of a breakdown in public order. Less than a month later a Peoples Democracy march from Belfast to Derry was savagely attacked at Burntollet Bridge in County Londonderry. Serious rioting broke out in the city and in a breakdown of discipline some policemen attacked shoppers in a city centre store. The possibility of containing the situation was becoming ever more remote.

MORE TOWN THAN GOWN

On Wednesday 15 January NICROC announced that it was to organise a demonstration in Northern Ireland on Saturday 25 January. They proposed to take a group of people from Oxford to Belfast and to march from the City Hall to the Stormont parliament building, a route which would take them through Protestant areas of East Belfast. They declared that they would not join with any local civil rights organisation, and that their party would be non-sectarian and represent opinion in England. Their claim was that Oxford people marching to Stormont could not be accused of any motive other than the promotion of civil rights.

The response in Belfast was predictable, and there were threats that the marchers would be tarred and feathered if they tried to go through Ballymacarret, a working-class loyalist area which lay on their route to Stormont. The march was banned by the Northern Ireland Minister of Home Affairs, Captain William Long. NICROC issued a statement asking how Captain Long could praise the Royal Ulster Constabulary for its efficiency, and, 'at the same time confess that it could not protect the peaceful procession of English visitors against the bully boys'.[17]

A Northern Ireland Civil Rights Association statement said, 'This latest in a long series of bans demonstrates once more the peculiar Unionist concept that the only way to prevent public disorder is to deny the right of free assembly'.[18] The Nationalist MP, Austin Currie, pointed out that British citizens were not being allowed the same rights as they had at home, and added, 'The ban demonstrates once again that British democracy does not exist here'.[19] The Peoples Democracy issued a statement pledging their full support for the NICROC action. They said that they did not intend to participate. It was clear, they said:

> that even a group of people from England who are uncommitted to any party or religion [sic] group in Northern Ireland will be prevented from exercising a democratic right to march, which they would be allowed anywhere else in the UK ... Any disorder that the Government anticipates can only come from Unionist extremists

attempting to hinder the march. The ban is therefore an indication that they are unable or unwilling to keep order among their own supporters.[20]

The Oxford protesters attracted the attention of one of the most prominent opponents of the civil rights movement, Major Ronald Bunting. The Major, a former British Army officer, has slipped from historical memory but in the late 1960s he was nearly as notorious as Ian Paisley. Bunting was a mathematics instructor in Belfast Technical College and had at one time been a supporter of Gerry Fitt. But he came under Paisley's influence and emerged as a pugnacious loyalist leader. He was jailed along with Paisley for leading a mob which occupied the centre of Armagh city, to block a civil rights march. He also took it upon himself to 'harass and harry' the Peoples Democracy march from Belfast to Derry in early January 1969. On 24 January Major Bunting said that his organisation, the Loyal Citizens of Ulster, would mount a counter demonstration to the NICROC one, at which they would demand 'civil rights for Roman Catholics, including the rights for priests to marry, the right of women to family planning methods and the right of Roman Catholics to refuse to pay for escape from Purgatory'.[21]

The NICROC party of around 50 was undaunted. Mary Holland in *The Observer* described them as 'a mild looking bunch anxious to emphasise that they were more town than gown'.[22] The delegation included students from the University and Ruskin College, Young Liberals and factory workers. They travelled to Liverpool where they boarded the *Ulster Queen*. The main spokesperson was Joe Fanning, the Secretary of NICROC, a Dublin-born draughtsman and a Ruskin student. Before leaving he had phoned the Home Office to ask for a reply to a telegram he sent to the Home Secretary, James Callaghan, asking for protection. He was told that Callaghan had taken no action on the matter and the Home Office officials did not know when he would be in a position to do so.

On arrival in Belfast on the morning of Saturday 25 January the NICROC delegation was greeted at the ferry terminal building by Major Bunting. 'Good morning Oxford group', he said:

> Welcome to Northern Ireland and be good. We hope you are not going
> to give any trouble or incitement to the people of Northern Ireland.
> The people here are amiable and virtuous, but they do not welcome
> interference from busybodies and long haired intellectuals. You do not
> look like law breakers, but we are watching you carefully. We offer you
> the hand of friendship which you may throw aside, but we may have
> another hand.[23]

After breakfast a four person delegation was sent to negotiate with
the police, who agreed to allow a meeting outside the City Hall.
There the NICROC speeches were drowned out by counter-
demonstrators. Afterwards the Oxford delegation walked between
placard-waving, jeering, counter-demonstrators who sang, 'go
home you bums'. They made their way to Queen's University
accompanied by police and followed by a tail of counter-demonstrators. They were diverted away from Shaftesbury Square, where
a crowd of loyalists from nearby Sandy Row were waiting for
them. They arrived at the Student's Union building where there
were a few scuffles and eggs were thrown by loyalist counter-
demonstrators. The Oxford demonstrators invited their opponents
into the meeting; the invitation was refused and the loyalists were
nonplussed when the Oxford group started singing 'God Save the
Queen'. The visitors then took part in a teach-in on civil rights in
the Union's McMordie Hall with no further trouble. After a heated
discussion they decided not to defy the Home Affairs Minister's
ban, and abandoned their original plan to march to Stormont.

On returning to the Donegall Quay ferry terminal that evening
they were met by about two dozen opponents who had managed
to get inside the building before the police could exclude them. A
further counter-demonstration of about one hundred stood
outside. The *Irish News* reported:

> The group [of counter-demonstrators] inside, mainly followers of the
> Rev. Ian Paisley and Mr. Ronald Bunting hurled abuse at three
> members of the NICROC who stood in the foyer to ensure their party
> arrived safely. The verbal attacks covered the Catholic Church, the
> Irish emigration situation, standards of living in the Republic and the
> housing situation in Derry city.

One of the NICROC officers was hustled upstairs by a policeman when he jovially held out his hand to demonstrators who were offering contributions to the cost of a gallon of petrol for a young Derry man who had threatened to set fire to himself because Derry Corporation has not been able to provide a house for his family.[24]

On leaving Belfast a NICROC spokesperson compared their treatment with the response of the Oxford authorities to their demonstration the previous November. He denounced the ban as '... ridiculous. Only the people who came from Oxford have been taking part. There have been plenty of stewards and I cannot see how we could have caused disorder.'[25]

NICROC claimed that they were going to organise a follow up demonstration of up to 400 from Birmingham, Manchester and other cities. This never materialised, but the Committee did organise a number of large meetings in the Blackfriars Dominican Priory in central Oxford, at which leaders of the civil rights movement like Ivan Cooper, Bowes Egan and Bernadette Devlin spoke. A large amount of money was raised and much of it was spent on giving holidays in Oxford to children from Northern Ireland. A family was brought over and given money and a caravan but there were disputes within NICROC about this strategy; the former treasurer, Mick Henry, disagreed with it and he resented the way in which meetings were dominated by the Communist Party. [26]

This episode is of some interest. In later years a perception grew up that the civil rights movement had been hammered into the ground every time it tried peaceful protest. This impression is gained by running together the march in Derry on 5 October 1968, the ambush at Burntollet of the Peoples Democracy march from Belfast to Derry in early January 1969, and Bloody Sunday in Derry on 30 January 1972. But between the first two episodes there were no less than eight civil rights marches at which a combination of effective stewarding and fair policing prevented violence from taking place; these included some of the largest civil rights marches and demonstrations of civil disobedience that ever took place.

There was one major civil rights demonstration between the Burntollet march and the NICROC intervention; it took place in

Newry on 11 January 1969. Violence broke out, but this time it was from civil rights supporters who attacked police tenders. On two occasions, in late 1968 and early 1969, civil rights marchers were subject to physical attacks by loyalist opponents during cross-country marches, at Magheramason on the border of counties Tyrone and Derry on 26 October 1968, and at Burntollet Bridge, near Claudy in Co. Derry, on 4 January 1969. On both occasions there was evidence that the RUC had been negligent in protecting the marchers.

In their pamphlet about the Burntollet ambush, Bowes Egan and Vincent McCormack proved that a high proportion of the attackers were 'B' Specials.[27] They would have had arms training and legally-held firearms. This is to say nothing of the guns which are normally available in the homes of country people. But brutal as the attacks were, these firearms were not used. Instead the attacks involved the use of sticks and stones at Magheramason, and stones, iron bars, and cudgels with nails in them at Burntollet. The Ulster Volunteer Force had gunned down a young Catholic barman in Belfast in June 1966, but in 1969 the NICROC marchers were threatened with tar and feathers, not bullets.

There were real fears of violence in this period. When Gerry Fitt said at the Oxford rally the previous November that there might be serious loss of life he seems to have had in mind the kind of spontaneous communal conflict which did break out in August 1969. The NICROC demonstration shows that in January there were still significant restraints on violence. The civil rights movement and its supporters, which included many people who later joined the Provisional Republican Movement, were committed to peaceful protest, and compromised on a number of occasions to avoid violent confrontation. The authorities were unwilling to allow complete freedom of demonstration, but the police did protect the NICROC meeting in front of the City Hall, a location which had been banned to anti-Unionist demonstrators up until the previous October. The loyalists were more willing to use violence, but were constrained in the type of violence which they offered.

The story of the NICROC expedition to Belfast confirms the

need to distinguish between the civil rights phase of the troubles and the later phase of armed conflict. It also helps to distinguish between the violence which occurred in the period of the civil rights campaign and that of the 1970s, when the Provisional IRA campaign and loyalist counter-violence had begun. In *Politics in the Streets* I tried to show the flaws in the case made by those who have accused the civil rights movement of being a conspiracy to bring about the destruction of Northern Ireland. The evidence of the NICROC episode underlines the point that, although the civil rights campaign unintentionally helped to create the conditions in which the bloodshed of the last twenty-five years occurred, it cannot be blamed for that bloodshed.

SINGING GREENSLEEVES

As I write this, the wall opposite the College, in Worcester Place, still bears the faded remains of a slogan: 'IRA Bastards'. This was painted by right-wing opponents in the late 1970s, when some students supported Republican insurgency against the British government. But in 1969 students were motivated by the kind of ideals which led to the demonstrations outside 'Annette'. They saw the Northern Ireland question in terms of discrimination and denial of equal rights, in other words as an extension of the anti-racist campaigns which led to the arrests at 'Annette'.

Civil rights in Northern Ireland is now associated with the violence of the Northern Ireland troubles, but at the time it was seen as a moderate cause. Liberal public opinion in Britain was solidly on the side of the civil rights movement. The Northern Ireland Home Affairs Minister, William Craig, who had ordered the ban on the 5 October march in Derry, made things worse by a tendentious attack on the Civil Rights Association. On 7 October *The Guardian* editorialised:

> The Minister for Home Affairs yesterday chose to describe the behaviour of the Londonderry police ... as 'discreet'. This is fantasy. What kind of discretion is it which results in over 30 marchers (including one MP) being treated in hospital while only two policemen are hurt? If the

police practise is to strike obstructive demonstrators on the legs, as Mr. Craig claims, how did heads happen to be bleeding?

The London *Times* of the same date said: 'His assurance that the police used no undue force echoes exactly that of Mayor Daley in Chicago last month'.

In November 1968, by a vote of 13 to 7 and after a heated debate, Oxford Trades Council defeated a motion denouncing the police for searching demonstrators on buses going to 27 October Vietnam march. But at the same meeting, unanimously and without discussion, they passed a resolution in support of the NICROC march in Oxford. The first was proposed by Joe Richards, a Communist and one of the English trade unionists who went to Belfast; the second was proposed by Mick Leahy who initiated the idea of the trip to Northern Ireland.

The Northern Ireland civil rights movement hoped to rally British public opinion against the Unionist government and it tried to appeal to the liberal consensus in Britain. There was a large degree of idealisation in this. Dr Conn McCluskey of the earliest of the civil rights groups in Northern Ireland, the Campaign for Social Justice, said, 'my heroes are all the people who belong to the British National Council of Civil Liberties who are democrats and liberals and who have something we Irish haven't, a bit of objectivity'.[28] Ian Leighton, a Ruskin student who had grown up in Coleraine, Northern Ireland, wrote about the Northern Ireland Civil Rights Association, 'Here ... was an association which was not concerned with the old sectarian differences ... but simply with the rights of man'.[29]

NICROC was attempting to appeal to this liberal opinion which the civil rights movement believed could swing the balance against the Unionist government. They even told Kevin Boyle of the Peoples Democracy that they intended to carry a union flag on the march. The heading on their leaflet, 'Have You Thought About Your Country Lately?' left open the question of whether the 'country' was Ireland or Britain. Mick Henry remembers that the demonstrators were urged to try to appear 'as English as possible'. This meant that they were not to drink on the boat and not to sing Irish songs. He proposed singing *Greensleeves*.

In fact most of them were Irish or of Irish extraction. The architect of their tactics was Mick Leahy, a veteran Irish nationalist who was a member of Oxford Trades Council and sympathetic to the Communist Party. He was in close touch with Betty Sinclair, the Secretary of Belfast Trades Council and Chairman of the Northern Ireland Civil Rights Association. She was a well known Communist and also a voice for restraint; she initially opposed the proposals for civil rights marches. Joe Fanning was a Communist and as Secretary of NICROC helped to carry the Party 'line'. Despite their studied moderation, however, Communist control of the Committee helped to alienate Irish working-class people in Oxford and it lost the support it had gained in its early days.

I have identified three Ruskin students who took part in the NICROC demonstration – Gerry Doyle, Tony Rosato and Joe Fanning. Doyle was from Vulcan Street in east Belfast, an active member of the Northern Ireland Labour Party and a former member of the Executive of the National Union of Seamen. On the outbreak of violence in August 1969 he returned to Belfast to look after his family and he participated in efforts to quieten sectarian animosities and to work for peace. Tony Rosato was from south Belfast, a militant Republican and a supporter of the 'Marxist' Official movement after the 1970 split. Fanning was from Malahide, Co. Dublin, a Communist and a member of the Draughtsmens and Allied Technicians Association. All three had a personal interest in the issue, and the bulk of the radical left in the College were not as intensely involved. But Ruskin was again important as a catalyst. It brought politically experienced Irish students to Oxford, it offered a venue for the NICROC rally in November 1968, and many Ruskin students took part in the demonstration in Oxford.

FEAR ... MILL NOT MARCUSE

In linking town and gown in direct action Ruskin students of the late 1960s reflected essentially liberal ideas about racism and democracy. Their leaflet for the strike against racism on 1 May 1968 said 'Immigrants are *not* to blame for unemployment, bad housing, overcrowded schools and hospitals and the decline in living standards'. In the leaflet for the 8 June teach-in they said, 'It is clear that we shall all live, for the rest of our lives, in what will be in some sort a multi-racial society. The nature of that society depends on what is done *now* during its formative years'. These sentiments reflected the integrationist approach of Martin Luther King, not the Black separatism of Stokely Carmichael.

In 1968 and 1969 they understood the Northern Ireland situation in terms of democracy and discrimination, not as a revolutionary struggle for national liberation. And in opposing racism it was the moderation of their demands, confronted by the obduracy of authority, which provoked their radical, direct action, tactics. There were other ways in which their radicalism was limited. Many left-wing students were hostile to the History Workshop movement and to its conference on women's history which helped to launch the women's movement. These have been the most enduring contributions the College has made to radical causes in Britain.

And despite the rhetoric of the 'red bases' strategists, the ORSS and the wider student movement shared many of these inconsistencies. The then President of the National Union of Students, Trevor Fisk, summed it up in 1969 when he commented: 'The basic feelings which spark off unrest are normally a sense of outrage when the College authorities offend not Marxist tenets but what students see as fundamental humanitarian liberties. Vice Chancellors still have more to fear from Mill than from Marcuse.'[30]

In 1909 Ruskin students rebelled against the College authorities and led a movement which had long lasting effects on the political and educational ideology of the British labour movement. But it was prompted as much by loyalty to their Principal Denis Hird, and frustration at not being listened to, as by opposition to capitalism. Their strike was followed by reform of the College and the adult educational system, and not by the social revolution which they had imagined. Their counterparts sixty years later took part in a long forgotten protest, but which was consistent with the ideals of their predecessors. It deserves to be remembered.

NOTES

1. *Oxford Mail*, 28 October 1968.
2. *Oxford Times*, 24 May 1968.
3. 16 October 1968.
4. 22 October 1968.
5. *Oxford Times*, 15 November 1968.
6. Minutes, 30 January 1969.
7. Telephone interview, 28 May 1999.
8. *Oxford Times*, 3 May 1968.
9. *Oxford Times*, 24 May 1968.
10. 28 June 1968.
11. Email to Bob Purdie, 15 May 1999.
12. For an account of the car factory at this time see Alan Thornett, *From Militancy to Marxism*, Left View Books, London 1987.
13. See my 'Internationalism and the Civil Rights Movement. An Epitaph' in Eve Patten (ed), *Returning to Ourselves*, Belfast 1995.
14. 15 October 1968.
15. Bob Purdie, *Politics in the Streets*, Blackstaff, Belfast 1990.
16. *Oxford Times*, 6 December 1968.
17. *Irish Times*, 24 January 1969.
18. *Ibid.*
19. *Ibid.*
20. *Irish News*, 25 January 1969.
21. *Irish Times*, 25 January 1969. Major Bunting had a personal tragedy in later years. His son Ronald joined the civil rights movement, and through that eventually found his way to the Irish Republican Socialist Party. The son was murdered in October 1980.
22. 26 January 1969.
23. *Irish Times*, 27 January 1969.
24. 27 January 1969.
25. *Ibid.*
26. Interview, Oxford, 21 May 1999.
27. *Burntollet* LRS, London 1969.
28. W. H. Van Voris, *Violence in Ulster: an Oral Documentary*, Amherst 1975, p53.
29. *New Epoch* (Ruskin magazine), 1970, p22.
30. 'The Nature & Causes of Student Unrest' in *The Political Quarterly*, Vol.40, 1969, p424.

Left apart: Raphael Samuel, David Selbourne and the crisis of the left in the 1980s

GEOFF ANDREWS

Ruskin's dissenting traditions have provided the backdrop to many different voices. Notably this has included the site for the first Women's Liberation Movement conference in 1970, the lynchpin of many progressive movements, including anti-colonial ones, trade union action groups and civil rights support networks. Therefore to describe it as merely the 'working-class Eton', a kind of feeder for the trade union movement, is to miss the breadth and complexity of its political significance.[1] It may be the 'college of the labour movement', but its political allegiances during the time I was a student in the mid-1980s extended far beyond orthodoxy, with the fair sprinkling of social movement activists, communists and Trotskyists reflected in the various representative and activist bodies. Students were more likely to leave than join the Labour Party, with their 'labourist' inclinations more likely to be challenged by critical and heretical positions than reinforced by norms. The different loyalties that characterised Ruskin's relationship with the labour movement, its situation as a college committed to academic excellence for adults and its explicit attempt to offer an alternative philosophy of education brought many tensions (not all of them creative). This meant that it was 'an exciting but dangerous place to be', as well as a unique, if complex, institution.[2]

This is an account of Ruskin's most prominent dissidents amongst the teaching staff, Raphael Samuel and David Selbourne.

The nature of their dissenting relationship to the College mirrored some of Ruskin's own paradoxes in its relationship to the university – at times, outsiders looking in with a critical eye at existing traditions. Both Samuel and Selbourne maintained a critical detachment from some of the College's traditions and, particularly in their early years at the College in the 1960s, challenged its status, arguing for more student participation, the radicalisation of its syllabus, and the promotion of more egalitarian educational philosophies.

Both Selbourne and Samuel were unconventional academics. Both had made a particular commitment to Ruskin, when they might have pursued a more orthodox academic career elsewhere, for its alternative radical status and the particular experiences and background of its students. Both sought a wider public audience for their work, writing frequently for the national press, notably in the 1980s in the *Guardian Agenda* pages or the *New Statesman*. It was an added source of interest for students – and motivation if preparing for tutorials – to keep up with their latest article, often on the fortunes of the left. Their unconventionality was also reflected in their mode of work; Samuel, the founder of the History Workshop, was committed to 'history from below'; the emphasis here being on the gathering and illuminating of hidden, fragmentary experiences and memories. Selbourne in the 1980s, on the other hand, turned increasingly to journalism, where his observations and judgements helped to interrogate some of the major political and social upheavals of the time; his application of theoretical insight gave further meaning to contemporary dilemmas, the predicaments of the left increasingly becoming the dominant theme of his work.

These approaches were important in understanding their political identities in the 1980s; Samuel, the 'keeper' of popular heritage and left faith; Selbourne, increasingly the heretic, on the look-out for uncomfortable and inconvenient truths.[3] These two notable public intellectuals were as distant as could be imagined from the contemporary academic world of the 'career bureaucrat' and 'research hermit'. Both had shared broadly 'new left' rather than labourist backgrounds; Samuel was one of the pioneers of the first New Left in Britain; and Selbourne moved from liberal dissenter to Marxist in the 1960s. This brought them close in the political context of the period both within and beyond Ruskin.

The focus of this chapter however is the way in which their dissent went in different directions during the critical period of left decline in the 1980s.[4] During this time they both remained critics of accepted wisdom but were now talking different languages of dissent. Samuel revisited traditional left values in the face of what he saw as an abandonment of principle, faith and allegiance in the pre-New Labour modernisation trends; a phenomenon he described as 'post-radical chic' and among whose adherents he included Selbourne himself. It was during the mid-1980s that he saw, at an early stage, the problems that would follow from the view that modernisation should carry all before it. He was particularly concerned with the way in which history and tradition were swept aside in the rush for new perspectives. He began to feel increasingly that the class loyalties, human dignity and experience of working people were being rendered obsolete as economic decay, unemployment and technological change was used as justification to reshape social and political agendas.

For Selbourne on the other hand, the 1980s took him on a rather different journey. In his words he found it increasingly difficult to 'square my own long-standing ('left') sentiment and conviction with the inconvenient truths ...' of his observations of contemporary Britain. His journalism for *New Society* took him to some of the major sites of change: Ray Honeyford and multiculturalism in Bradford; Militant Tendency's control of Liverpool City Council; poverty and ill-health in Lancashire; the South Yorkshire coalfields and the problems facing the black community in the Midlands.[5] As events unfolded they began to confirm to him the severity of left decline, the continuing inability of left ideas to gain conviction amongst those whom it had always considered its natural constituency. He found that its analyses were flawed and its solutions were now not only seen as undesirable, by newly affluent groups, but 'utopian'. The 1980s for Selbourne provided the evidence that the left had become irretrievably removed from everyday experiences and aspirations. In his writings, both in the theoretical analysis set out in *Against Socialist Illusion: A Radical Argument* and in his journalism, he began to interrogate the sacred cows of the left in a style that won him few friends and identified him as the most prominent dissident within the ranks of the left. Like Samuel, perhaps, he was also ahead of his time in identifying the faultlines of the new political era; for him, however, the need to break with left traditions and uncover the illusory aspects of left-wing discourse were paramount; the unsentimental harshness of his tone was as distinctive as the sympathetic idealism of his colleague.

THE LEFT IN THE 1980s

The problems confronting the left in the 1980s have been well documented and can be found in the variety of 'rethinking left' books and articles, as well as in the more humorous accounts such as John O'Farrell's confessional memoirs of a Labour supporter, *Things Can Only Get Better*. The themes underlining most of these focus on the implications of the decline of traditional manufacturing industry, the fragmentation of class loyalties, as well as numerous psephological and sociological explanations of Labour's worst ever performance in General Elections. Above all, the working class 'ceased to be largely Labour', to use Ivor Crewe's phrase, and the consequences of this were manifest in weakening class identities, new 'individualistic' aspirations and new forms of consumer satisfaction. That it was the right that benefited most from these developments was in itself a shock which the left was ill-prepared for; after all many continued to believe that the economic crisis which emerged in the 1970s could only have one outcome, namely the swing to socialism.

Of course not everything about the 1980s was depressing for the left. The rise of new social movements provided new sources of emancipatory politics, released from some of the more conservative constraints of labour movement cultures. The turn towards civil society rather than the state as the empowering vehicle of justice and equality could also be seen as a sign of left optimism, epitomised most of all by the Ken Livingstone-led Greater London Council. The Campaign for Nuclear Disarmament also had a brief reincarnation, and the Women's Peace Camps at

Greenham Common pioneered a new form of protest. Yet these developments also seemed to question, as much as confirm, the validity of the traditional left.

As a consequence, some of the disputes that were played out in the 1980s in retrospect have an almost surreal dimension; the flying mass pickets coinciding with the rise in share-ownership; greater demands for loyalty and solidarity among trade union and left organisations at the same time as large numbers of working-class people deserted the cause in favour of individual aspirations. The activism on the left appeared almost as manic as the degree of passivity from the non-activist majority, while the language and culture of the left started to appear at odds with people's everyday experience.

Because of the nature of Ruskin and the unique composition of its student body, there was a particular significance attached to these events. Between 1983 and 1985, the years I spent as a student, the key moments of the period contained a complex mixture of hopes and fears. The great struggles which, in retrospect, can be seen as marking the end of an era of industrial struggles, included the mass picket at Warrington on 30 November 1983, against Eddie Shah's use of non-union labour, through to the miners' strike (1984-85), where Ruskin played host to miners from Merthyr Vale Lodge. These struggles, which largely delineated the political parameters at Ruskin, symbolised the extent of difficulty facing the left. Disagreement over strategy was a constant reminder that it was not merely a lack of solidarity that needed to be addressed (though this itself was a cause for conflict), but an understanding of the wider difficulties of sustaining traditional types of protest in a period of post-industrialisation.

More hopeful signs were Livingstone's GLC, which signified the emergence of new kinds of radical politics and which gave impetus to the non-Labourist Left. Hopes of finally defeating Apartheid were raised by the release of David Kitson, a long-term political prisoner and former Ruskin student, while the Peace Movement remained an important source of left identity.[6] These pessimistic and optimistic currents coexisted uncertainly, drawing out conflicts and loyalties in the student community that would not be found in any other educational institution, but which were microcosms of the left and labour movement as a whole. Thus Ruskin students were victims of picket-line violence and false arrest, played (as at other times) key roles in Miners Support Groups and social movements, and probably had over-generous bouts of optimism as well as suffering from illusions.[7] My Ruskin cohort was defined by the end of traditional trade union hegemony and the political culture associated with it, revealed in different ways in the disputes within the student body – over the importance of class, the significance of feminism, black sections in the Labour Party, the treatment of Peter Tatchell in the Bermondsey by-election, the merits of 'municipal socialism' (in David Blunkett's Sheffield as well as London) and the division in the Communist Party, between the 'Euros' and the 'Tankies'.[8] Against this background, though, there was a particular concern for the bigger picture: 'Whither the Left' was the underlying question for many of us and seemed to dominate many personal exchanges and conversations.

THE HERETIC

This doubt over left predicaments was reinforced by the political influences and 'interventions' of those who taught us. By the mid-1980s David Selbourne was becoming increasingly dissatisfied with the left's inability to recognise either the scale of its intellectual decline, or the nature and extent of the right's appeal. Together with many others on the left at the time (for example *Marxism Today*), he thought the crisis was deep-rooted. His critique went further than most however and included a frank reappraisal of the whole worldview of the left, to the extent that it was found wanting on even its most basic values. Even the key organising principles – socialism, the working class, the left itself – needed to be put in quotation marks, such was their ambiguity and scale of misuse.[9]

The extent of his pessimism often resulted in the misleading assumption that there had been a simple shift to the right on his part, perhaps because of the sheer verbosity and harshness of his polemics, which interrogated the full range of left shibboleths. As one reviewer of his work put it: 'He seemed to be applying the most exacting standards to the Left while giving the Right a softer tutorial'.[10] However, such an interpretation is not borne out by his lecture programmes where the radical causes – the diggers being a particular favourite – were given prime attention; his targets those of privilege and reaction. The Labour Party and its labourist culture, whether in the form of contradictory philosophies or trade union conservatism, were a particular target; a situation which, in fact, continued to endear him to the left, while ruffling the traditional Labourites, who were threatened both by his political polemic and the depth of his theoretical critique.

Increasingly Selbourne found that the long-held assumptions of the left (particularly those held by left-wing intellectuals) were becoming redundant in the face of existing realities and everyday experience. Essentially he argued that there was a schism between the popular aspirations and expectations of the population and the political discourse and culture of the left. Thus the left was increasingly found to be holding 'illusory' expectations about the prospects for socialism, a situation that in the conditions of the 1980s was particularly disastrous. In *Against Socialist Illusion*, published in 1985, Selbourne argued that

> the lingering expectation that the socialist alternative can be revived around the old political constituency, and around the old constellation of socialist ideas, however refurbished ... needs to be firmly resisted. To promote illusions which have already failed, or projects which time and circumstance are in the process of disqualifying, is merely to block the path for genuinely new forms of radical critique of our world and its institutions.[11]

At the heart of this illusion was the failure to recognise the contradictory aspects of the left's positions, and above all the inability to distinguish 'progress' from 'reaction' in many of the crucial economic, social and political events that were unfolding. Moreover the Labour Party – the main target of his attack – was unable to grasp the true nature of what was going on because of its own ideological make-up; its 'broad church' including pro- and anti-capitalists, grassroots activists and statist centralisers.

A further problem, he argued, was the way in which what he called the 'private interests' of labour served to undermine any socialist case and to obscure further the contradictory postures of trade union leaders; they substituted industrial militancy for political radicalism and were committed not to the overhaul of the capitalist system but to preserving its inherent social relations. The failure to recognise these contradictions meant that the left would never break out of its decay and the important questions would remain unresolved.

> In the political culture of the market, the trade unions are above all the brokers of the private interests of labour, the producing class, and not the opponents of the capitalist system. Brokerage is their social and economic function: they could not avoid it even if they chose to; and they do not choose to. That is, labour organisation in a market society furnishes the collective or social means to the end of individual appropriation of economic and social goods, however precarious, and labour, like capital, is not the less a private interest for organising itself socially in the labour market by the only effective means available to it.[12]

For Selbourne there were depressing consequences to be derived from this. It meant that even in some of the most militant struggles of the 1980s that had emerged in response to the technological and market-driven priorities of employers, the 'private interests of labour' prevented a 'progressive' response. The Wapping dispute for example was less a conflict between 'progressive' trade unionism and 'reactionary' management than 'the trade unions semi-feudal insistence upon job property rights in expiring, or defunct, forms of the division of labour ... Likewise in this technologically revolutionary period, the left does not dare to admit that it is predominantly labour, not capital, which has become what Marx called a "fetter on the forces of production"'.[13] He wrote this piece at a time in 1986 when his own lectures were boycotted for effectively crossing the Wapping picket line by writing an article for *The Times*, an event which eventually precipitated his departure from the College some four months later.

Another consequence of the private interests of labour was that the ideological framework which organised the agenda of British socialism was intricately bound up with an inherent contradiction; it simultaneously wanted the end of capitalism while depending on the system's economic prosperity for its programmes, leading to what he called 'socialism for good times'; that is, one where the core social programmes were reliant on a prosperous capitalist economy and the inevitable social relations that went with it. This meant that its core ideas of equality and liberty were inevitably disabled in periods of economic crisis, which he saw as crucial in giving purchase to the agendas of the New Right. The New Right built its intellectual platform on precisely these paradoxes over the meaning and application of freedom and equality; the guile of Friedman and Hayek in rooting their critique in the experience of the post-war welfare state was a theme of his tutorials.

He argued that, with the left mistakenly attributing its predicament to a range of factors such as media conspiracy, lack of resolve, or fickleness of the masses, the reasons why the (new) Right was able to take power in the conditions of capitalist crisis, high unemployment and social decay were obscured. Recent experience and popular cultural perceptions were undoing the ideological premises of the left. Thus the left's interpretation of equality became identified with what was generally perceived as either unobtainable or undesirable due to its effects on personal liberty. Freedom itself, on the other hand, had a stronger legitimacy in its attachment to those liberal individual values that the left had underplayed:

> In our popular political culture, 'liberty' has much more to do with claims to individual economic independence than the fond prospect of socialist transformation; while 'equality' has above all signified equal citizen rights (including to private property), and equality of opportunity rather than of outcome.[14]

Against the background of the real or perceived failures of 'actually existing socialism' and social democracy, the ideological legitimacy of the right increased; it was no good the left arguing that the market and freedom were mutually exclusive or that 'real freedom' could only be attained under socialism. He went on:

it is because neither equality of circumstance, nor opportunity, nor outcome is attainable – if attainable at all – in a capitalist market society, and because none of them is ideologically perceived to have been attained in 'real' socialism either, that the right's objections to the pursuit of equality tout court have taken on a sufficient plausibility to earn them a comfortably-sustained ideological approval.[15]

It was in this context that Selbourne began to contest in very public ways – as well as in his teaching – the ideological basis that underpinned the main totems of the left. Comprehensive education, for example, could never be the 'socialist oyster in the capitalist shell', by transforming social relations through the classroom. The prevention of council house sales, he argued, was a tactical error which was probably the biggest single reason why Labour lost the 1983 election; it represented a failure to identify with these popular aspirations for self-fulfilment.

RESISTING POST-RADICAL CHIC

Raphael Samuel was one of the young turks of the first New Left, a movement distinguished by its critical engagement with modernity, its alternative view of modernisation to that offered by Wilsonite technocracy and its pioneering concern with popular culture. In 1956 he was one of those who opposed the Soviet invasion of Hungary and took on board Kruschev's revelations about Stalin. In the 1980s his political identification became repositioned as a defender of tradition, questioning the drive towards modernisation of the labour movement and defending the 'classical' values of solidarity, the dignity of labour and a 'sense of worth' – values he saw as under threat from a range of sources, which included the first signs of labour modernisation, the rise of the Social Democratic Party (SDP) as a response (or capitulation) to the market philosophy of Thatcherism. He was above all concerned with the social 'costs' of modernisation, the dispensing of historical narrative in political argument and the view – which has now become as mainstream in contemporary political discourse as in business ethics – that modernisation has an unchallengeable authority.

This did not mean that Samuel was classic 'Old Left', let alone 'Old Labour'. He resisted the easy postures of many in the 1980s whose revolutionary politics didn't extend beyond the student union or the armchair and whose delusions were interrogated by Selbourne. Indeed the consequences of the deep divisions on the left at this time were a recurring theme for Samuel as much as for Selbourne. The miners' strike of 1984-85, for example, 'highlighted the ideological collapse of both social democracy and communism when faced on the one hand with the renewed vitality of capitalism as a world system and, on the other, with the ... loss of jobs'.[16] The strike, he argued, 'cruelly exposed the limitations of a purely oppositional trade unionism', in its defensive mode, unable to think strategically about the nature of decision-making, or about questions of investment, the possibility of worker participation and alternatives to the 'right to manage' philosophy that was dominant. Nor did he underestimate the particular ideological appeal of Thatcherism, noting Thatcher's ability to 'make complex issues seem transparent, and translate the mysteries of statecraft into the vernacular of everyday life ... Prosaic little sayings are inflated into categorical moral imperatives. Ideology is domesticated as home truth'.[17]

Samuel's view was that the miners' strike was symptomatic of the divisions on the left. The left had been pushed onto the defensive, was variously 'simmering with doubt', 'embarrassed into silence', or, in the case of the Labour Party, was afraid of guilt-by-association. 'The miners' strike', he wrote in an angry preface to his co-authored collection of essays, *The Enemy Within*, 'serv[ed] as a displaced object of the left's discomfort with itself, of a Communist Party which is no longer certain what it exists for, of a Labour Party which is no longer sure what it believes in, of a New Left which has lost its taste for the streets'.[18] One outcome of this uncertainty on the left was the audacity and growing confidence of 'post-radical chic'. This was typified above all by the move away from class and its association with traditional socialist principles, as well as providing further justification for 'new realism', the forerunner of what was to be New Labour's particular take on modernisation. These problems were most prevalent in the more journalistic accounts, which, lacking the insights of the historian, to Samuel were 'melodramatic', with a prediliction for 'events' rather than 'processes', and focusing excessively on the personal failings of Arthur Scargill.

What was missing in these accounts for Samuel, whose conviction was reinforced by numerous visits made to the South Wales Coalfield as well as long discussions with the miners resident at Ruskin, was a recognition of the sacrifice and energy behind the strike. In the scrum to write the obituary of the mines, there was a denial of the amount of commitment communities had to muster in what was a 'very unequal struggle'. It was, he said, a display of 'an exceptional sense of worth', of 'collective self-regard'. 'The strike was an act of faith – faith in each other, faith in the unions, faith in their leaders, faith in coal as a bedrock of British life'.[19]

In talking of the 'very majesty' of the strikers' efforts, Samuel risked – and in the case of Selbourne amongst others received – criticisms of romantic and illusory perceptions. Yet the strike had unearthed new forms of solidarity – in the case of the Women against Pit Closures and Gay and Lesbians Support the Miners. To overlook these events was to rob communities of hope and to deny efforts of survival.

For Samuel, those that had written off the miners and who were quick to see in their defeat confirmation that left principles were irreparably flawed, or that the distinction between left and right was becoming obscured, or that new social constituencies were becoming more important than traditional class loyalties, or that economic decline meant an inevitable victory for the right – a curious complement to left versions of revolutionary defeatism which took hold in the 1980s – were mistaken. The main reason for this wrong interpretation, he argued, was the preference for novelty and imagery over sober, historical reflection, the deference to media driven agendas. The response to the miners' defeat was indicative of a wider political shift, where acting out of conviction, standing up for principle, was now deemed out of date.

This 'post-radical chic' was a phenomenon without substance; a cosmetic fad which, although at times supported with reference to philosophical or sociological interpretation, was too often driven by a need for drama, making up in presentation what it lacked in principle. A classic example of this was the Social Democratic Party's

(SDP) adoption of R.H. Tawney as their spiritual guru. Being brought up on Tawney himself, Samuel admitted to 'indignance' at the SDP's attempted appropriation of the former; he regarded it as 'an afterthought, an exercise in generating fictitious moral capital rather than the acknowledgement of a spiritual debt'. Samuel noted that David Owen's *Face the Future* made only one reference to Tawney and Bill Rogers' *The Politics of Change* none at all. Samuel's comparison between Tawney and the SDP found little to justify the connection. In the case of Roy Jenkins, for example ('a part-time banker' who was given to a 'sensuous delight in political in-fighting and parliamentary management, metropolitan dinner parties and society gossip'), there was little to unite the latter's 'patrician' and 'Whig' outlook with the ethical socialism of Tawney.[20]

In general the SDP's 'inflation of the new', 'devaluation of the past', its 'populism' and rejection of 'outdated dogmas', was contrasted with Tawney's 'epic sense of the past', his principled ideological and ethical opposition to capitalism and his 'humanitarian indignation' at privatised self-interest. The SDP's radicalism was a 'secular' and Americanised affair, with no sense of social justice or a principled cause.

> Where Tawney was apt to see violently opposed moral and ideological imperatives, the SDP argues that all the great questions are negotiable, if they can be defused of their ideological charge. It is thus possible to advance women's rights without raising the issue of feminism, to promote equality while treating the idea of socialism as old hat, to bring the two sides of industry together while leaving the structure of ownership unchanged'.[21]

THE CONFUSIONS OF CLASS POLITICS

For David Selbourne perceptions of class as well as changing class formations were at the root of the decline in the fortunes of the left during the 1980s. In the midst of the dislocation between the organised politics of the left and the labour movement and the working class was a series of misconceptions about class identity. One side of this was what he saw as the confusion between 'proletarian' and 'plebeian' cultures, where an uncritical identification with some of the populist strands of mass opinion was elevated into class consciousness. Within the left – that by its nature has to seek 'mass' support and puts its faith in the 'masses' to achieve its historic mission – illusions over the extent of consciousness, mistaken interpretations of struggle, and misunderstandings of the real aspirations of ordinary people were commonplace for Selbourne. In this crisis of class identity what he saw as 'plebeian' values were frequently amplified as part of proletarian virtue. Thus he equated the activities of the pickets in the miners' strike with the culture of football terraces – 'the stamping ground of the plebeian' – and the posturing of the Militant Tendency in Liverpool was 'lumpen street Trotskyism', a workerist culture in which personal appearance, language and lifestyle were in themselves raised to revolutionary potential by virtue of 'not being middle class'.[22]

In another direction he found that many of the problems facing the left could be located in the disjuncture between real working-class aspirations and a middle-class socialist politics, in which imposed notions of working-class identity, the 'human-as-worker' for example, obscured popular aspirations, while simultaneously mistaking defensive sectional interest for class consciousness.

The 'crisis of the working class movement' is as much the crisis of intellectual failure to grasp its true nature as the crisis of 'the movement itself'. To impute to 'the working class' and its alleged defects of 'consciousness', responsibility for the failure of the socialist project (and its projectors) is to deepen every illusion. Indeed to use fundamentally middle-class concepts of the working class and the 'proletariat' as the organising principles of socialist theory and practice is to have been at odds from the beginning with the self-identification of 'working' people themselves, whether as citizens, appropriators, consumers or individuals.[23]

Moreover the illusions of middle-class socialist intellectuals contrasted unfavourably with the more 'down to earth' perceptions of those on the right who struck a chord, he argued, with these same popular aspirations; and this was in spite of a tendency amongst some on the left to reinvent themselves as 'honorary proletarians', his term for workerism. Indeed the key terrain that distinguished the left from right in many of these exchanges was the latter's better grasp of the construction of, and attention to common sense, a concept best articulated in the work of Gramsc but which became appropriated in the 1980s by the more 'organic intellectuals of the right. For Selbourne, then,

> To compose, for the purpose of socialist analysis, an abstract prole tariat from real human beings is one thing; to confine the real humar being, for the same purpose, to the human-as-worker, is another; bu to make consciousness of class the highest criterion of authenticity o response-to-life in the human-as-worker (but in no-one else) is a fina reduction of the nature of human activity, experience and knowledge.[2]

An even more revealing manifestation of these dilemmas was the middle-class socialist view of the nature of work itself. Here, unlike many other non-socialist writers (including Matthew Arnold and Oscar Wilde), the left was guilty (according to Selbourne) of seeing only the virtuous and 'dignified' side of work, which did not match with working-class experience. Where the middle-class socialist intellectual – and he included Raphael Samuel in this particular group – saw only admiration, dignity and virtue in manual work, to others such work was demeaning, monotonous and dirty. Therefore, while for the (Marxist) intellectual labour was the key to emancipation, for many workers themselves as well as some non socialists, work was something from which to escape. To argue for the 'right to work' he argued was not only in the short term the 'right to work for capital and for the state which manages its inter ests', but in the long run the basis for continued drudgery. It also missed the point, he suggested, which was that the working class has shown more inclination in seeking emancipation through the need 'to escape, not to control, the means of production'.[25]

THE CONTINUING RELEVANCE OF CLASS

In contrast to this, Raphael Samuel's critique of what can now be seen as the forerunners to modernisation was shaped to a large degree by what he saw as the abandonment of the traditional working class, an aversion to talking about the experiences and struggles of social groups whose lives and work were being transformed. The social 'costs' of modernity were, above all, class factors – the political and social communities that had been shaped by class alignment and what he called 'class feeling'. The perception of a more 'classless' or more 'middle class' oriented society was beginning to dominate, and was the main impetus behind the new political agendas, notably the growth of the SDP, the conflicts within the Communist Party as it played out its final drama from the mid to late 1980s, and the overall shifts that clearly pre-figured the rise of New Labour.

Samuel, along with other writers such as Beatrix Campbell and Jeremy Seabrook, as well as the magazine *New Society* which, under the editorship of Paul Barker, ran regular series of social documentaries on the changing reality of working-class communities, tried to get into the experiences and relate subjective responses to structural change and political identity. He saw the changes within the nature of the middle class as being equally as important as those amongst working-class groups. In a series of articles in *New Socialist* he compared the 'new middle classes' with those of an earlier period, the middle classes between the wars. Between the wars, the middle classes were 'less a class than a society of orders', in which 'keeping up appearances' was paramount in maintaining a fixed social status based upon distance and snobbery, in respect of clearly defined and threatening social 'others', the working class and, specifically, the labour movement.[26]

This middle-class identity was 'constituted amid a sea of social fears, with hidden reefs on which the frail barque of respectability could only too easily be wrecked.' The 'new middle class' in the 1980s was less insular and more 'meritocratic'. It's 'repressed energies had been released' in the liberalisation of the 1960s and it had become more 'sociable' and outward looking and more diverse and inclusive in deciding who should enter its ranks.[27] It knew how to enjoy itself more, favouring 'instant' rather than 'deferred' gratification and was more confident in its mission to provide political and cultural leadership.

The Social Democratic Party, founded in 1981, was the clearest expression of the political voice of the new middle class. It had recruited its members from what he called 'frustrated professionals'; the 'administratively minded intellectuals, educational technocrats, fainthearted feminists, career politicians ... one time progressives and ideas men enjoying a second youth'.[28] The social composition of the SDP, with 57 per cent of its membership from professional and managerial classes and a 'remarkable number of former student politicians among them', was crucial to its identity. The image of modernity that it projected through a relentless show of novelty and obsession with style was another way in which it organised its distinctive agendas. In this respect, according to Samuel, it described its approach as 'flexible' as opposed to 'rigid', 'clear-thinking' rather than 'dogmatic' and 'radical, but reasonable'.[29] What defined its identity more than anything else, he said, was its class location, a 'newly unified middle class', which, seeing the old status divisions as unimportant, assumed itself – wrongly – to be the arbiter of a 'new classlessness'. Rather, Samuel argued, its distinction from the working-class population was crucial in the way it defined itself. This was clear in its hostility to the ghettoised council estates, its rejection of the culture of organised labour and its distaste for working-class habits, making it 'much too fastidious', Samuel suggested, 'to touch a man who is beery'. Indeed, for Samuel, they wanted 'to abolish the working class', as confirmation that society could be reformed without specific claims to community. Their leaders didn't come from the ranks of the labour movement, or the public schools, but 'characteristically from nowhere ... and positively rejoice in the absence of regional or local ties'. This, he argued, was indicative of a 'delighted act of self-recognition by a new class coming out and discovering its common identity'.[30]

If the rise of the SDP signified the emergence of the new middle class then the dispute in the Communist Party of Great Britain, between 'Eurocommunists' and 'tankies', which reached its peak in the mid-1980s, signalled to Samuel the crisis of working-class politics. Indeed the splits inside the Party for Samuel had less to do with the 'Russian question' than with 'the condition of England' question, with the 'break up of class loyalties' and other 'sociological discomforts' comprising the underlying dynamics of the division.[31] Eurocommunists, of a different generation, were seeking distance from the traditional loyalties of the labour and working-class movement as a pre-condition for renewal. This was reflected in their attacks – not unlike Selbourne's – on what they saw as 'economism' and 'workerism', and their preference for new social movements. *Marxism Today*, as the mouthpiece of this position, was largely to blame; its editor, Samuel remarked, had taken on the status of a minor media celebrity.

In his three part series in *New Left Review* Samuel, in reflecting on what he described as the 'lost world of British communism', saw 'class feeling' as the lynchpin of the Communist Party's entire existence. Historically the ability to maintain its organic working-class links with the trade unions set it apart from other communist parties, and the dominance in its social composition of the engineers in particular, and other skilled workers, gave it a strong socio-cultural focus as well as the belief that it was delivering the historic mission of the proletariat. The socio-cultural factors included a distinctive 'proletarian morality' and identity, which influenced the behaviour of the party's members, its codes of conduct, its public face and self-image. From his communist background and the particular influence of his mother and her comrades in the 1930s and 1940s, Samuel recalled the centrality of the language of class in the way in which the Party went about its business. The importance of class impinged on most aspects of the party's life, including attitudes towards 'clean living', condemnation of excessive drinking, the virtues of respectability and the importance given to self-education. If the rise of the SDP then was synonymous of the emergence of a new middle-class politics, the decline of the Communist Party was the sign of the end of a particular type of working-class politics.

RESURFACING: THE TWO TRAJECTORIES AND CONTEMPORARY DILEMMAS

The responses of David Selbourne and Raphael Samuel to the crisis of the left in the 1980s, around the themes of left values and class identity, carry a significance beyond their diverging paths. The circumstances of Selbourne's departure from the College in 1986 in a much publicised dispute seemed to reflect some of these diverging positions about the place for liberal dissent and the collective ties of solidarity.[32]

The degree of their political differences can be gleaned further from their response to the end of Communism, which became a focus in different ways in the late 1980s. Samuel's *New Left Review* articles revisited Communist Party traditions and lamented the decline of the culture and ethos of the party, first brought to him by his mother and her contemporaries in his own Jewish communist upbringing. For Selbourne, the reaction was quite different. In the period after his departure from Ruskin he travelled to eastern Europe and found himself caught up with the momentous changes taking place. In *Death of the Dark Hero* he provided an explanation through his own observations and the voices and experiences of those he encountered; the events had very clear consequences, he suggested, for the future of socialism, as well as being for him a kind of personal liberation in which he rediscovered his Jewish identity:

> Now, yet more rooms in the Utopian mansion of socialism have fallen. Proletarianism, East and West, and the politics pursued in its name, has proved to be one of the world's curses. Labour and the politics of labour, not capital, has been shown – from Wapping to Warsaw – to be the true fetter on the forces of production. It is capital, not Das Kapital, which the States of eastern Europe require in order to release the pent-up energies of their people.[33]

The wider significance lies in the two trajectories that have divided the left in recent years and continue to provide a focus for many political debates. On the one hand, the need to modernise, to escape from the trappings of the past, to fully come to terms with the failures and to reconstruct a new political culture, by identifying new social constituencies and re-positioning a new political 'project', has become mainstream as the path chosen by New Labour. Many of the heretical positions first taken by Selbourne, which made him such a hated figure in some areas of the left, have now been accepted as given; among them are reform of the trade unions, the importance of individual freedom and the removal of equality as the organising principle of the left. This would locate his work within the growing constituency of 'beyond left and right'; a third-wayer from the time when only two roads seemed plausible. His later work saw a connection between his 'modernising' path and that taken by the New Labour government. His book *The Principle of Duty* was given a high public profile, circulated to MPs and quoted with approval by President Clinton; a situation that reflects the rather unlikely outcome of finding him more in tune with received opinion. It may be that, in his quest to be completely free of the trappings of left ideology, articulated in his most recent work through the emphasis on duty and community, he has left himself in more ambiguous territory; the more mainstream communitarian agenda with which he is now associated lacks a critical cutting edge; its cultural conservatism is unable to engage with the pace of techno-logical and social change.

Raphael Samuel, on the other hand, represents a different perspective. Described by Selbourne himself in his *Observer* obituary in 1996 as the 'conscience of the old left', Samuel's arguments, while often perceived as out of place with the harsh realities of 1980s revisionism, still serve as a crucial rejoinder to rampant modernisation, in an era in which political principle fares badly against gloss and imagery.[34] His questioning of the pace of modernisation, the antipathy towards history and tradition, and the costs of economic and technological change on communities, continues to pose a critical message to those that judge on the basis of focus groups and think tanks. His critique of the SDP holds good for New Labour, who seem to have adopted large chunks of the former's policy agenda – pro-Europe, in favour of constitutional reform, affirming the need to break the mould and develop meritocratic 'classless' constituencies. New Labour's reliance on professionals and imagery, its complete ease with media networks, closely follows the direction of the SDP.

We should be wary however of reducing Samuel and Selbourne's work to these two positions. It would be as absurd to reduce Samuel entirely to the persona of Old Labour as it would to identify Selbourne solely with New Labour, particularly as he has already completed a critique of it, albeit for a right-wing think tank.[35] Samuel, on the other hand, took up enthusiastically the call for a national history curriculum in the late 1980s, making important contributions to the debate, extending his concern for heritage and the importance of historical engagement. It would be as well in an era of managerialism and conformity, in which the parameters of critical intellectual engagement have become increasingly narrow – both within and beyond higher education – to recognise their contributions as dissidents, as public intellectuals who did not follow convention easily and who always sought the wider spaces and the bigger picture.

NOTES

1. *Observer*, 27.6.99.
2. R. Samuel, *Guardian*, 16.10.86.
3. B. Schwarz, Raphael Samuel obituary, *Guardian*, 10.12.96.
4. This shouldn't suggest there was a simple shift from agreement to disagreement between them, but that the areas of difference were initially narrower. See, as one example, Selbourne's critique of the methods of the History Workshop and Samuel's response: *History Workshop Journal*, spring 1980, pp150-176; a complex debate which takes place within Marxist historiography.
5. D. Selbourne, *Left Behind: Journeys Into British Politics*, Cape 1987, pix.
6. David Kitson was released in the summer of 1985 and immediately took up a position as a tutor in mathematics and statistics, offered to him by the College while in Prison. The author was secretary of the Ruskin Kitson Committee at the time of his release, later re-named the Kitson-Mandela Committee.
7. As an example of the way in which left discourse was seen as more ambiguous, a friend and Ruskin contemporary, Phil Henshaw, was arrested for using the word 'scab' on a miners' picket line.
8. Jim Mortimer, then General Secretary of the Labour Party, accused Peter Tatchell of being 'ostentatious' about his homosexuality in a speech at Ruskin in late 1983.
9. D. Selbourne, *Prefatory Note Against Socialist Illusion: A Radical Argument*, MacMillan 1985, p1.

10. Martin Kettle, *Guardian*, 16.2.93.
11. D. Selbourne, 1985, *op.cit.*, p28.
12. *Ibid.*, p158.
13. D. Selbourne, 'The Strike of Angry Passion', *Guardian*, 2.6.86.
14. D. Selbourne, 1985 *op.cit.*, p39.
15. *Ibid.*, p65.
16. R. Samuel, *New Socialist*, October 1986, p16.
17. R. Samuel, *New Socialist*, April 1985, p5.
18. R. Samuel, *New Socialist*, April 1985, p7.
19. *Ibid.*, p15.
20. R. Samuel, *Island Stories*, Verso, pp234-235.
21. *Ibid.*, p243.
22. D. Selbourne, 1987 *op.cit.*, p155.
23. D. Selbourne, 1985 *op.cit.*, p70.
24. *Ibid.*, p77.
25. *Ibid.*, pp85, 90.
26. R. Samuel, *New Socialist*, Jan/Feb 1983, p30.
27. R. Samuel, *Island Stories*, pp257, 259.
28. *Ibid.*
29. *Ibid.*, p263.
30. *Ibid.*, pp271; 270; 263.
31. R. Samuel, 'The Lost World of British Communism', *New Left Review*, September-October 1987, p55.
32. The dispute over Selbourne's departure was well chronicled in the pages of the *Guardian* at the time: see Hugo Young, 'Unquiet Goes the Don', 14.10.86; and Raphael Samuel's response 16.10.86: 'Ruskin College and the Stones of Unfairness'; the letters pages carried the story for days afterwards. See also P. Hirst in *New Statesman*, 24.10.86 and J. Lloyd in *New Statesman*, 31.10.86.
33. D. Selbourne, *Death of a Dark Hero*, Jonathan Cape 1990, px.
34. D. Selbourne, *Observer*, 15 December 1996.
35. D. Selbourne, *One Year On*, Centre For Policy Studies, 1998.

Counting the cost: Financial hardship and second chance students

RICHARD BRYANT

Our first efforts must be to help individuals who can escape their situation to do so, in the knowledge that personal skills and employment are the most effective anti-poverty policy in the long run. This is why the top priorities of our government are welfare to work and tackling the problems of bad schools and low educational standards.[1]

Widening participation in further and higher education is one strand in the Labour government's policies to modernise the welfare state and promote social inclusion. Central to this project is a commitment to develop new learning, training and employment opportunities for those groups who have long occupied a marginal position in post school education and the labour market – e.g. unskilled and unemployed workers, lone parents and women on low incomes, black and ethnic minority groups, disaffected young adults and people with literacy difficulties. These groups have represented, over many years, a key part of the student constituency for Ruskin and the other long term Residential Colleges.

The rhetoric which currently informs policies and debates about participation and social inclusion represents an apparent shift in politics and social policy – a move away from the silence about the structural causes of poverty and the blaming of victims which characterised the Thatcher and Major years. On the other hand, serious doubts have been expressed as to whether the promise of this policy shift can be fulfilled without income redistribution through the tax system and a renewed emphasis upon the citizen's entitlement for state support, as well as their responsibility to help themselves.[2] In the case of widening participation in post school education, the acid test will be in the policies which inform the funding support arrangements for students. For many mature and second chance students their experience of further and higher education is comparable to an obstacle course of Grand National proportions. Self confidence has to be developed, writing skills polished up or acquired, academic language demystified and personal and family relations re-ordered. For all but the affluent, there is the further obstacle – the Beechers Brook of the course – that is represented by the demands of financial and economic survival. What should be an adventure in self-discovery can easily become a careworn journey, beset by worries about money and debt.

This chapter reviews the impact of financial pressures on full time Ruskin students – with particular reference to students on the College's Social Work courses – and highlights how the funding policies of successive governments have shaped student experience and continue to pose critical issues for the future role and scope of Ruskin's contribution to adult education. The evidence about student's experiences mainly derives from course and college wide surveys conducted by Applied Social Studies tutors, between 1979-98.

APPLIED SOCIAL STUDIES

For people who think of Ruskin as being synonymous with trade union education it may come as a surprise to discover that the College has been running vocational courses, for social workers, for over thirty six years and that there is evidence of Ruskin students preparing for careers in social work from as early as the inter-war years. Pollins records that, from the late 1920s, students attended lectures on social work at Barnett House (Oxford University) and that 'a few students also undertook practical work so as to obtain their Social Training Certificate'.[3] Barnett House, along with the London School of Economics, was a pioneer in the development of

British social work education and the links, which were made by students in the 1920s, established an association between Ruskin and the Oxford University course which remains to this day. Further evidence of social work interest, during the inter-war years, is provided by a 1936 survey of the activities of former students – out of the 111 former students who responded 26 were classified as being employed in social work and welfare, compared with 19 trade union officials and 21 in education.[4] The College's Applied Social Studies courses started in 1963, with the setting up of a one year Residential Child Care course (RCC), which was subsequently transformed into a two year Certificate Qualification in Social Work (CQSW) in 1973 and which, in turn, became the Diploma in Social Work (Dip.SW) in 1993. During the same period, a one-year pre-professional course – the Certificate in Community and Youth Work (CCYW) – was also established. In the academic year 1998/99 students on the social and community work courses comprised over a quarter of college's full time students – 52 (42 Dip.SW, 10 CCYW) out of a total of 179.

Vocational education at Ruskin has always had two major aims: to provide education and training for working-class women and men who have previously been denied, or have missed out on, educational opportunities; and, secondly, to offer a vocational training within a learning environment which is committed to the philosophy that intellectual stimulation, academic adventure and political challenge are integral elements in the preparation for becoming a social or community worker. Underpinning these aims is the assumption that the life experiences and informal learning of the students provides a basis of know how, social commitment and transferable skills which can be invaluable in working with disadvantaged individuals and groups, and which is rarely matched by younger students who enter social or community work through graduate routes.[5]

LEARNING IN POVERTY

During the period when data has been compiled on student funding – 1979 to 1998 – the annual intake on the two year social work course varied between 15 and 25 students and the financial support available for students covered two distinct sets of arrangements. Between the late 1970s and the early 1990s students on the CQSW course were mainly funded by discretionary LEA grant awards. From 1991 this was replaced, in relation to the new Dip.SW/Dip.HE course, by a mix of mandatory grants awards and loans. This system will in turn be replaced, from 1999-2000, by the Labour government's scheme of 100 per cent loans and means tested tuition fees. Over the same twenty year period the majority of Ruskin students, who are on non-social work courses (including the CCYW students), have been funded by mandatory grants from the Department of Education – Adult Education Bursaries (AEBs). The AEB funded students were on two-year courses until 1993, when the current one year Certificate in Higher Education course was introduced.

In the 1999-2000 academic year the maximum personal maintenance grant for an AEB student, who is not eligible for any additional allowances (e.g. dependant's grant), is £2886 for a thirty eight week year, while the maximum loan available to a student in similar circumstances on the Dip.SW programme is £3635 for a fifty two week year. For a student who is resident in college the cost of their board and accommodation, over three terms, is £2100 – leaving a AEB student with £786 or £20.50 a week for other expenditure and a Dip.SW student £1535 or £29.50 a week. A person aged 25 and over, with no dependants, on Income Support would receive £51.40 a week plus housing benefit.

What trends have emerged from the long term monitoring of the finances of students on the Ruskin social work and the AEB funded courses? During the late 1970s and early 1980s around a third of the students on the social work course reported having incurred debts as a direct result of undertaking their education and training at Ruskin and, by the late 1980s, this figure had doubled to 66 per cent. A 1989 survey of the full time students at the eight long-term Residential Colleges indicated that the incidence of debt on the Ruskin Social Work course reflected the experiences of AEB students on other two year courses – with 60 per cent of students at Residential Colleges reporting course related debt.[6] With the exception of Coleg Harlech (83 per cent), the Ruskin students recorded the highest incidence of debt (64 per cent).

The increase of course related debt on the Ruskin social work course during the 1980s, and the debt levels recorded by AEB funded students in the late 1980s, reflected the impact of the Conservative government's education and welfare policies – including cutbacks in local authority expenditure, the erosion of secondments to social work courses, the pegging back of the value of grants in relation to increases in the costs of living and the withdrawal of a range of welfare benefits from students in the mid-1980s.[7] The cuts in welfare benefits included ending the eligibility of students to claim Supplementary Benefit and Unemployment Benefit in the short vacations and ending the eligibility to claim Housing Benefit for students paying rent to an educational establishment – a measure which had a particular impact upon students at the Residential Colleges. Underpinning these cuts and changes in student support was the Thatcherite philosophy of 'removing students from dependence on social security' and fostering financial self reliance – aims which were to dominate government policies towards full time students for the rest of the century.[8]

During the 1990s the incidence of social work students reporting course related debt has steadily increased, hovering around the 75 per cent mark for most of the decade and peaking at 92 per cent in 1998. Between 1990-1994 the incidence of debt reported by AEB funded students varied between 72-81 per cent and had fallen to 52 per cent by 1996, following the replacement of two-year courses by the new one-year Cert. HE course. The key factor which accounted for the increase in course related debt on the social work course was the introduction of student loans. In the face of widespread opposition, the 1990 legislation (Education Student Loans Act) brought in loans for all full time students in higher education – with the exception of post graduates – and also introduced a phased freezing in the value of maintenance grants. This legislation also completed the process of ending welfare benefit entitlements for most full time students. From the start of the 1990-91 academic year full time students, with the exception of lone parents and people with disabilities, lost their remaining entitlements to Income Support, Housing and Unemployment Benefit. This loss of benefits also applied to the AEB funded students, although they were not covered by the new loan scheme. To compound the problems, for some older students, the mature student's allowance was abolished in 1995. For those students aged 26 and over who qualified for the allowance – just over 50 per cent of all Ruskin full time students at the time – this cut represented a loss of over £1000 in the value of their awards.[9]

The recent Labour government's legislation on student support arrangements – (Teaching and Higher Education Act 1998) – replaced the previous mix of loans and grants and free tuition with a 100 per cent loans scheme and means tested tuition fees. These new arrangements, which will be being fully implemented in the 1999-2000 academic year, effectively complete the process which the Thatcher government embarked upon in the mid-1980s, although even a Conservative government was reluctant to completely abolish maintenance grants and end universal free full time education by means testing tuition fees. Despite a vigorous lobby from Central Council for Education in Social Work (CCETSW), social work teachers and the British Association of Social Workers (BASW), the Government refused to exempt Dip.SW courses from the new arrangements and grant social work students the same status as students on initial teaching training and nursing courses, who will continue to receive bursary awards and free tuition. The DfEE explained the decision to make special arrangements for teachers and nurses on the grounds that 'it has direct employment responsibilities and a key interest in maintaining a healthy supply of labour in these professions' and added that 'it cannot take responsibility for the supply of those professionals who are employed predominantly in the private sector'.[10] The DfEE had – either out of ignorance or political convenience – disregarded the available information about the outcomes of social work education. Research by CCETSW into the employment of qualifying social students indicates that, over the five years between 1992-97, 85 per cent entered the public sector, with 10 per cent joining the voluntary sector and 2 per cent the private sector.[11]

Although most of the political and media attention directed at the Labour legislation has focused on the controversy surrounding the introduction of tuition fees, a more pressing issue for students from low income households is the loss of the remaining maintenance grant. In 1999-2000, 22 per cent of second year students on the Ruskin social work course will be liable to pay a full or partial fee contribution, whereas over 80 per cent of the intake will lose grant awards of over £800. Maintenance awards, because they are means tested, favour students from lower income households. This key point was clearly recognised by Dearing in the National Committee of Inquiry into Higher Education, but was ignored by the Labour government. Dearing concluded that to abolish grants and completely replace them with loans 'takes away subsidies from the poorer families and provides more substantial loans to others.'[12]

Alongside the increase in the incidence of course related debt, there has been an increase in the size of the debts incurred. During the late 1970s and early 1980s, the majority of those students who incurred debts were reporting amounts in £100-£500 range. By the end of the 1980s the average debt incurred at the end of the course was £750 and this had increased to £3000 by the middle of the 1990s. In 1998 the average debt was £3500, with a small number of students reporting debts of over £10,000. The main creditors were banks and financial institutions (including the Student Loan Company), families and friends. For the AEB funded students the size of debts has been reduced since the introduction of the one-year courses. In 1996 the majority of AEB funded students who had course related debts reported amounts of between £500-1000. With the introduction of the 100 per cent loan and means tested fees scheme the size of debts incurred by social work students will inevitably increase after 1999/2000. CCETSW has estimated that, depending on domestic circumstances, the debts incurred over the two years of a Dip.SW programme could be as high as £10,000 for a single student, £8500 for a married student and £15,000 for a lone parent.[13]

For many students at Ruskin, course related debt adds to financial commitments which are present before they enter further or higher education because, unlike younger students, mature and second chance students invariably bring with them a formidable range of household, family and child care responsibilities. The evidence suggests that the incidence of pre-course debt has increased over the years. In the late 1980s, a quarter of the students reported having debts (i.e., outstanding loans other than a mortgage) prior to starting the course and, by the mid-1990s, this had increased to over a third of the intake.[14]

The incidence and scale of debt on social work courses has a major impact upon women. At Ruskin women comprise around two thirds of the annual intake on the social work course, a figure which mirrors the national profile of students in social work education but which – with the exception of the Women's Studies programme – is far higher than the number of women on other Ruskin courses.[15] Amongst the students on the social work course, lone parents – almost exclusively women – report having the highest levels of financial commitments, when compared with students who are married/cohabiting or single students who are not supporting dependants. The financial commitments of lone parents are confirmed by the findings of national surveys of student finance. Callender and Kempson in their 1995/96 survey of 2000 students at seventy higher education institutions, concluded that:

> Regardless of their family circumstances, mature students owed the largest amounts so that, overall, they owed twice as much as younger ones. But, amongst mature students, lone parents stood out as having the highest levels of financial commitments – owing £3302 compared with the £1523 owed by younger students.[16]

One response to financial hardship and pressures is for students to take on paid employment during their course. The increase in the number of Ruskin students working, during term times and practice placements, has been very evident over the last twenty years. Throughout the late 1970s and the early 1980s a minority of the social work students (20 per cent) reported working during term time and practice placements. By the mid-1980s the number working had crept up to nearly a third and this had increased, for term times, to just over half by the end of the decade. The period between 1990-98 witnessed further increases, with two thirds of the students working during term time and a smaller number (55 per cent) working during practice placements. In 1998 students worked an average of between 11-15 hours per week, with a small number working between 21-31 hours. The main source of employment was with statutory, private and voluntary agencies, which provided residential and group care services – such as children's homes, senior citizens' homes and probation hostels. There was a time when CCETSW disapproved of social work students working during term times and placements and tutors counselled students about the risks they were running, in terms of the negative impact upon their studies and practice placements. Today, if a hard line was taken with students, the course could well experience a sharp reduction in applications. Working during term times is not confined to social work students. In 1996 just over a quarter of the AEB funded students reported working in term time – mainly in retail, catering and offices.

Debt and poverty has been a fact of life for Ruskin students over a long period of time. Since the mid-1980s, cuts in welfare benefits and the abolition of the mature student's allowance have made the situation worse for a majority of the College's full time students. The introduction of loans has had a direct and negative impact upon the financial circumstances of the students on the social work course. For many students working during term time and placements has become a necessity, as has borrowing from family, friends, banks and the Student Loan Company. Lone parents are particularly vulnerable to financial pressures and incurring debts. Those Ruskin students who are dependent on state support for their main source of income – whether in the form of loans or AEB bursaries – are living in poverty, as measured by a line based on Income Support scale rates.[17] Despite this, second chance and mature students are renowned for their commitment and fortitude. In the words of one AEB student:

> No matter what it takes I will continue to struggle till I get there.

At one level, Ruskin students appear to display the type of self reliance which successive governments have sought to foster amongst full time students. But what have been the educational and social costs involved in this process – for the individual student and the College?

EDUCATIONAL AND SOCIAL COSTS

There is clear evidence that financial pressures can adversely affect student's course work and studies and that, with the increase in the incidence and size of debt levels over the years, these pressures are now being experienced by a significant number of Ruskin students. In the late 1980s, 48 per cent of all the College's students reported that financial difficulties had affected their studies and, by the mid-1990s, this had increased to 67 per cent. Students frequently mention that they cannot afford to buy books and that financial worries distract them from their college work and undermine their motivation – resulting, in some cases, in them missing classes and essay deadlines and under-performing on their courses. Students who work during term time complain of difficulties in managing their time and being 'stressed out' with the constant juggling of college and work commitments, as these students' comments show:

> Learning and retaining knowledge requires a high level of concentration. Keeping one step in front of the bailiffs requires time and skill. Whilst in an educational environment, the mix of the two has resulted in stunted academic attainment. Why does being a mature student have to be so painful?

> ... Constant worry about paying off debts incurred means that I have to go home to stop spending any money. My grades dropped from B++ to B and I was not handing in essays on time.

> ... I get a grant of about £5000 but I still have to work. I need to earn about a £100 a month in term time, but obviously more in the holidays. It's a juggling job, working weekends and evenings, paying for some child care and working it out with friends at other times. I have taken out a loan this year but I'm reluctant to next year as I will have to start paying it back and still keep up my earnings to pay my mortgage. They

want mature students on these courses and not people straight out of school, and inevitably mature students will have additional costs or will have given up jobs to do it. Without the grant doing this course would be impossible.

Research at Oxford Brookes University has indicated that students who work during term time fail, on average, three times as many course modules as those students who do not work during term times.[18] The majority of social work students also work during their practice placements, which extend for fifty days in the first year of the Dip.SW course and eighty days in the second year. Working during placements poses particular strains, as the time commitment tends to be more structured and demanding in comparison to college based studies. Students work, on average, between 35-37 hours per week on the placements, often incurring additional financial costs relating to travel costs and child care responsibilities. In the words of two Dip.SW students:

> On a social work course – which is emotionally as well as academically demanding – having to work is terrible. Doing a sleep over at a residential home, where I've had only four hours sleep, and then having to go to the placement is bad.
>
> … There are hidden costs on a social work course. I did a fifty-day placement at a youth project which involved a 56 mile trip every day. I had to be there in the evenings because that's when the young people were around, so I have to pay for child care.

Worries about debts, juggling with part time jobs and studies, and cutting back on essential items of expenditure (e.g. food) can have adverse effects on a student's health and their relationships with families and friends. In the mid-1990s, 56 per cent of Ruskin students reported that their financial circumstances had an impact upon their physical and mental well being – tiredness, stress, strains on family life and loss of self esteem were frequently mentioned.

> Financial pressure has consumed time and placed pressure on relationships and the quality of my partner's life. You lose your self esteem by asking for financial help from friends and relatives (AEB student).

I was prevented from travelling home for a family funeral because of financial hardship (AEB student).

My exhaustion resulted in me needing medical treatment. Then family difficulties developed, due to my lack of time, energy and patience. On one occasion, my doctor advised me to leave the course (Dip.SW student).

During the 1990s, the possible link between financial hardship and ill health amongst students has begun to receive more attention from researchers and educationalists. Boaden, in a study of social work students in Liverpool, identified students with dependants and child care commitments, almost exclusively women, as having incurred the highest incidence of course related debt and having also experienced the highest rate of health problems during their training.[19] More recently Roberts, in a study of undergraduates at two London universities, drew some disturbing conclusions about the impact of financial pressures on student health.

Students were on average twice as likely to be in poorer health than non-students of the same sex and age, when measured on physical vitality and psychological and social functioning. Poor mental health was linked to longer working hours outside university and difficulty in paying bills. Those considering abandoning study because of cash problems were likely to have poorer mental health, lower levels of social functioning and poorer physical health ... Most students with children, one in eleven of our sample, said that they had problems paying bills, with many in debt. The children inevitably face hardship too.[20]

Financial difficulties can exacerbate stresses and strains which are caused by the life experiences of some students – such as the anxieties and tensions produced by periods of long term unemployment, damaged family relations, homelessness and previous negative encounters with the education system. Although the Residential Colleges have the reputation of providing a relatively high level of support for students, when compared with larger colleges of further and higher education, they are not havens of security which provide a safety net for the financial and emotional difficulties experienced by students.[21] Indeed, it could be argued that the new funding and management regimes which have been introduced into further and higher education over the last ten years have eroded some of the traditional networks of support and resources which were available to students. For instance, at Ruskin funding constraints and managerialist priorities have resulted in a tendency to replace full time tutors, on retirement, with part time sessional staff, with the inevitable consequence of reducing the levels of tutor support available to students. A.H. Halsey's comments on how 'business models' have changed the relations between academics and the government of universities could equally be applied to the changes which have occurred in the relations between the management, staff and students of colleges.[22]

> What is perhaps least appreciated was that the rhetoric of business models and market relations – the language of customers, competition, efficiency gains, 'value for money' etc. – could be substituted for relations of trust.[23]

The combination of financial and social pressures can result in students questioning whether they should continue with their studies and the numbers admitting to having doubts have increased over the years. In the late 1980s, 18 per cent of all full time students considered leaving their courses at some stage in their time at Ruskin, and by the mid-1990s this had increased to 38 per cent.

> Occasionally I become despondent about my financial position. This causes blow it syndrome, which may endure for a week. At such times I stop working (AEB student).

> If I had realised the problems of trying to do the course, and look after the family, I would not have started. Why should anybody suffer financially for wanting to gain an education? (AEB student)

The majority of students who consider leaving do remain on their courses. In the case of the social work students – who experience the highest levels of debt in the College – the drop out rate is relatively low and has never been above 10 per cent during the 1990s. But for some students the prospect of incurring more debt can also deter them or make them 'think twice' about moving from Ruskin on to degree level courses. In the mid-1990s, 44 per cent of students reported that financial considerations – including the loans scheme -were having a negative effect on their motivation to continue with their studies.

> Financial difficulties have made me refuse offers of places on higher education courses (AEB student).

> I will probably not go on to higher education because of the financial penalty this will cause (AEB student).

> Loans will discourage people from applying for higher education (AEB student).

In the case of social work students the debts accumulated over the two years of their training can prompt doubts about pursuing a career in what is still a relatively low paid profession.

> Even when I do get a job I don't know how I will pay back the £8000 of outstanding debts. I expect to earn about £14,000 in my first job and pay back £125 a month. I was earning more than that eight years ago, when I was working off shore. I probably won't stay in social work (Dip.SW student).

How prospective students perceive the financial implications of entering further and higher education, and weigh up the likely costs and benefits, has major implications for recruitment and admissions. The messages from the research on finance and student participation in further and higher education makes very uncomfortable reading for a college like Ruskin, which traditionally has offered a second chance to mature students from those social classes which are under represented in further and higher education i.e., C2 (skilled manual) D (semi-skilled) and E (unskilled). Mature students incur, on average, twice as much course related debt as younger students and the highest debts are incurred by students from social classes D and E.[24] Research studies also suggest that attitudes towards student loans are influenced by social class, household composition, gender and race. Surveys of young people and access students indicate that students from social classes C2, D and E are more likely to be deterred by the prospect of loans than are students from classes A and B.[25] In addition, women are more likely to be deterred than men; students with dependants more than single students and black students more than white students. A recent report from the Further Education Funding Council, on a survey of a 1000 full time and part time students in further education, concluded that older students experienced the worst financial problems and were the least convinced about the financial return on their education.[26] As the Report stated:

> To secure wider participation, lower drop-out rates, higher achievement levels by alleviating widespread student hardship, the financial support system must prioritise the needs of the most vulnerable – adult students, especially those with children ... The greatest potential scope for widening participation is among older students. Policies need to acknowledge that they experience some of the worst financial problems and are unconvinced of the financial return on their education.

Much of the research on finance and student participation casts serious doubts on the key cultural assumptions which have underpinned both the Conservative and Labour government policies on the funding of full time students in higher education. Both governments have sought to legitimise loan based schemes by arguing that the use of credit is now an acceptable norm among all social groups and cite evidence of the growth in mortgage finance and the use of credit for 'everyday purposes' to support the loan policies.[27] The research, however, indicates that amongst lower income groups there is considerable resistance to the loans policy and that, within these groups, the use of credit and loans is restricted mainly to coping with money management difficulties rather than as a means for funding increased consumption, or, as in the case of the education market, funding improved educational opportunities.[28]

The social groups which are most resistant to loans and incur the highest debts when they enter further and higher education are the very groups which have comprised the traditional student constituency of Ruskin College. This is one factor which has contributed to the difficulties the College has experienced, over recent years, in recruiting students for the Dip.SW and the Cert.HE courses. In the case of the Dip.SW course the loan schemes have had a direct impact on prospective students. The introduction of the Conservatives' loan scheme in 1990-91 resulted in a 38 per cent reduction in applications for the course and the applications for the 1999/2000 intake – the year when Labour's 100 per cent loans and means tested fees scheme is fully implemented – have fallen by 27 per cent, including a marked decline in applications from black candidates. The current fall in applications for the Dip.SW course reflects a nationwide reduction in the numbers of mature students applying for social work training and other higher education courses. In the case of the Cert.HE courses the College has experienced difficulties, in some years during the 1990s, in recruiting students to take up the full quota of AEB bursaries. Financial considerations – especially relating to concerns about incurring debts and older students being unconvinced about the financial returns of education – have been a factor in this situation, along with the expansion of access courses and the new educational opportunities for mature students provided by other colleges of further and higher education.

Financial hardship has significant educational and social costs for students and the College. The impact on students can include missing classes and under-achieving in their course work; problems with time management; stress and ill health and the disruption of personal and family relations. For the College, the financial pressures experienced by students can generate increased demands on tutors and administrative staff and can be a key influence on the ability of the institution to recruit and retain students.

FUTURE PROSPECTS

The Labour government, as part of the project to modernise the welfare state and promote social inclusion, has generated ambitious proposals to widen participation in further education and to promote lifelong learning which extends beyond colleges and embraces the workplace, home and local communities.[29] The long term residential colleges have been identified as having a role to play in this process:

> Their contribution to lifelong learning should be properly acknowledged and supported, with due recognition being given to the distinctiveness of their various missions and educational functions.[30]

Ruskin, which straddles further and higher education, has the history and potential to continue to make a significant contribution to adult education in the new century. Apart from the core work with full time students, the College has a long tradition of workplace education – linked with trade unions – community based education with voluntary organisations, and access provision for local residents in Oxfordshire. Also, in recent years, the College has introduced part time routes for the Cert.HE courses and, in the case of the Dip.SW, a part time work based route which has been developed in partnership with UNISON and Suffolk Social Services. Whether the fruits of these developments will be realised depends on appropriate resources being made available and on the financial support for full and part time students. Will the Government provide the same support arrangements for part time students as for full time students – as recommended by the Fryer Report – and will the shortcomings and inequalities of the loans scheme be recognised and addressed? The recent experience in higher education does not inspire confidence. A massive expansion in student numbers has been promoted, by successive governments, without the underpinning of an appropriate level of public funding.

> In 1998 David Blunkett, the Education and Employment Secretary, said that to fund higher education as it was twenty years ago would mean increasing income tax to 26p in the pound. But twenty years ago income tax was at this level and the UK had one of the most admired education systems in the world.[31]

The social cost of this expansion has largely fallen on the students and the impact is apparent in the growing incidence of debt, drop out, working during term times and ill health. Widening participation and inclusion in further and higher education will only become meaningful when students, especially those who have been previously marginalised by the education system and labour market, are considered by the state as valuable human resources and are rewarded, rather than punished, for their efforts. There are limits to self help.

> Can we have a decent living grant, so that we can enjoy and study in dignity? (AEB student).

NOTES

1. Peter Mandleson cited in R. Lister, 'From Equality to Social Inclusion: New Labour and the Welfare State', *Critical Social Policy*, Volume 18 (2), 1998.
2. *Ibid*.
3. H. Pollins, *The History of Ruskin College*, Ruskin College Library, Oxford 1984.
4. *Ibid*.
5. D. Statham, 'Open Letter to Martin Davies', *Community Care*, 12 December 1985.
6. R. Bryant and M. Noble, *Education on a Shoestring*, Ruskin College, Oxford 1989.
7. R. Bryant and M. Noble, 'Financial Hardship on CQSW Courses', *Social Work Education*, 6(1) 1986.
8. DHSS, *Reform of Social Security - Programme for Action*, Cmnd 9691, HMSO, London 1985.
9. L. Garner and R. Imeson, 'More Bricks in the Wall', *Journal of Access Studies*, Vol.11, 1996.
10. BASW, 'Loans decision may be based on ignorance', *Professional Social Work*, July 1998.
11. CCETSW, *Funding of Social Work Education and Training*, CCETSW, London 1997.
12. National Committee of Inquiry into Higher Education, *Higher Education in the Learning Society, The Dearing Report*', HMSO, London 1997.
13. CCETSW 1997, *op.cit.*.
14. R. Bryant, 'Why Does Being a Mature Student Have To Be So Painful?',

Adults Learning, May 1995.

15. CCETSW 1997, *op.cit.*

16. C. Callender and E. Kempson, *Student Finances; Income, Expenditure and the Take-up of Student Loans*, Policy Studies Institute, London 1996.

17. C. Oppenheim and L. Harker, *Poverty - The Facts*, Child Poverty Action Group, London 1996.

18. Oxford Brookes University, *The Effects of Paid Employment on Academic Performance of Full-Time Students in Higher Education*, University Academic Standards Committee, Oxford 1993.

19. M. Boaden, *Mature Student Finance*, Shelia Kay Fund and Liverpool Polytechnic, Liverpool 1991.

20. R. Roberts, 'Debts of Despair', *Guardian*, 2 February 1999.

21. A. Woodley, L. Wagner, M. Slowey, M. Hamilton and O. Fulton, *Choosing to Learn: Adults in Education*, The Society for Research into Higher Education and the Open University, Milton Keynes 1987.

22. A. H. Halsey, *Decline of Donnish Dominion*, Clarendon Press, Oxford 1995.

23. *Ibid..*

24. B. Redpath and N. Robus, *Mature Students' Incomings and Outgoings*, HMSO, London 1989; C. Callender and E. Kempson, 1996, *op.cit.*

25. K. Aughterson and K. Foley, *Opportunity Lost: A Survey of the Intentions and Attitudes of Young People as Affected by the Proposed System of Student Loans*, National Union of Students, London 1989; J.F. Bird and A. Baxter, *Access and Student Loans*, Department of Economic and Social Science, Bristol Polytechnic, Bristol 1989.

26. C. Callender, *The Hardship of Learning*, The Further Education Funding Council, Coventry 1999.

27. DES, *Top-Up Loans for Students*, HMSO, London 1988.

28. R. Berthoud, *Credit, Debt and Poverty*, Research Paper 1, Social Security Advisory Committee, HMSO, London 1989; National Consumer Council, *Credit and Debt: The Consumer Interest*, NCC, London 1990.

29. H. Kennedy, *Learning Works; Widening Participation in Further Education*, Further Education Funding Council, Coventry 1997; DfEE, *Learning for the 21st Century*, 'The Fryer report', DfEE, London 1998.

30. *Ibid.*

31. R. Roberts, 1990, *op.cit.*

Can Ruskin survive?

JANE THOMPSON

On 20 February 1999 Ruskin College celebrated its hundredth birthday. It was a glorious and emotional day, caught on camera in a mood of celebration, commitment and validation of Ruskin's presence in the world, and of its spirited affection in the hearts and minds of the former students and well wishers who attended the Centenary Gala in Oxford Town Hall. A hundred years earlier, photographs from the College archive show the same venue, packed from floor to ceiling with representatives of educational, co-operative, Christian socialist, labour and working-class movements – dressed in their Sunday best – together with liberal academics from the university, all keen to be associated with this new 'College of the People'.[1]

In 1899 the balconies were hung with British and American flags to signify the nationality of the College founders, Charles Beard, Walter Vrooman and Amne L. Grafflin. A hundred years later the seats were also full, the walls and balconies draped with the reminders of numerous socialist and feminist concerns, spanning a century of struggle by trade unions, women's peace campaigns, environmental groups, anti-racist and pro-democracy coalitions and the Labour Party.

Former students from as far back as the 1920s and 1930s mingled with those of the 1990s. MPs and trade unionists, Ruskin tutors and students contributed to the speeches. The Shirebrook Colliery Band played rousing and emotional music. Bad Habits, the women's choir, sang songs of protest from labour strikes and feminist campaigns. College tutors sold copies of their scholarly publications and students, old and new, queued up for tee shirts, mugs and mouse mats bearing the Ruskin logo, and to order copies of the Centenary video and music tape. Inside the main hall, the voice of John Prescott, the Deputy Prime Minister and Ruskin's most famous 'old boy', recounted memories of his first essay, 'Power Corrupts. Absolute Power Corrupts Absolutely. Discuss', and of being chased down the street by his tutor and mentor, Raphael Samuel, trying to persuade him to come back and finish the examination he had just stormed out of. Outside the hall, the lobby and exhibition area were crowded with conversation and reunions, as the sometimes famous and sometimes infamous reminded each other about where it all began.

At shortly after six, the Shirebrook Colliery Band led the assembled gathering, carrying banners and flaming torches, through the streets of Oxford and back to the steps of Ruskin, for one more chorus of the Red Flag, before the evening celebrations continued in party atmosphere, lasting until the early hours of the next morning.

Caught up in the exuberance of the occasion, with much evidence of energy, social purpose and credentials, it was hard to imagine that Ruskin might not survive, or that the Ruskin being celebrated – so warmly and with such passion – might be a figment of individual memories, memories involving selection, interpretation and invention, memories constructed in the present, in the complex interplay between individuals, to provide a collective account of the past. And this past was being created from a mix of personal histories, different political preoccupations, shifting expressions of identity, cultural meanings and emotional understanding, as well as structural and material circumstances linked to social class, gender and ethnicity – some of which have a lot to do with Ruskin and some of which have nothing to do with Ruskin. Together they produce ideas and assumptions about 'common interests and understandings' which attribute to 'the Ruskin experience' a kind of recognised consensus and solidarity. In practice this is likely to be an experience which is more diverse and contradictory than collective 'moments of being', such as the centenary celebrations, appear to suggest, but the centenary provides a way of thinking about historical connections, interrogating present contradictions, and imagining future possibilities.

Many would take the view that if Ruskin could survive eighteen years of Thatcherite conservatism, it ought to be able to survive the advent of New Labour – and not only survive but flourish. Especially with an old boy in the number two position. Tony Blair has indicated that 'Education. Education. Education' is a major government commitment. David Blunkett, Secretary of State for Education and Employment, knows about adult education and residential colleges like Ruskin from his involvement, as leader of Sheffield City Council, in the setting up of Northern College in 1978. Derek Gladwin, the Ruskin Chair of Governors until 1999, is active in the House of Lords, alongside Jack Ashley, Betty Lockwood and Bill McCarthy, all former Ruskin students. Both Prescott and Blair have made speeches at the College, and Andrew Smith, Minister for Employment in the DfEE, is a long time friend of Ruskin, and local MP for East Oxford.

If Ruskin is not exactly a household name, people involved in politics and education are likely to know more about Ruskin than about any other of the residential colleges, or almost any other further education college or new university outside their local area. It might be, as Hilda Kean suggests, that some if not most of this knowledge is coloured by a variety of myths created and perpetuated in the process of Ruskin inventing its own history of itself – from slippery, selected and contradictory accounts of numerous and various realities.[2] Nonetheless, the college has acquired the connections and the kind of reputation which other much bigger but less famous educational institutions would be happy to replicate.

At one time, this might have been enough to guarantee the college's survival. In the 1945 Labour landslide, thirteen former students were Labour MPs, and in the case of two others, Grace Coleman was once a Ruskin tutor and Arthur Creech Jones was a member of the Governing Council. The Prime Minister, Clem Attlee, had lectured at the College. Jack Lawson was a cabinet minister, and another minister, Philip Noel-Baker, had been vice principal. Between 1950 and 1979 the College Principal was Billy Hughes, who was a Labour MP in the Attlee government (before losing his seat to Enoch Powell), where he had exercised considerable influence as parliamentary private secretary to Ellen

Wilkinson, Minister of Education. His deputy and successor, John Hughes, was Deputy Chairman of the Price Commission, a member of the Industrial Development Advisory Board, and had strong contacts with both the Labour Party (John Prescott used to babysit Hughes's children when he was a Ruskin student) and leading trade unions.

In 1976 Prime Minister James Callaghan made a famous speech at Ruskin, which he recalled during the 1999 centenary celebrations as one 'which opened up a very necessary discussion about the future and purpose of education – a debate that is not finished yet'.[3] Tony Blair chose the twentieth anniversary of Callaghan's intervention to deliver a keynote address from Ruskin to a national audience about education in the run up to the 1997 election. However, reversing the old cliché, it is not simply who you know but also what you know that matters, in present circumstances – and whether what you know has any relevance or importance to those who might want to learn about it, given that Ruskin's historic commitment has been to individuals previously excluded from serious education, belonging to groups that have collective interest in progressive social change, as well as academic self improvement.

Ruskin has been more than occasionally associated with important developments in working-class education. In 1908 the Oxford Report on working class education was the first of five major twentieth century reports dealing with adult education in England and Wales (see pp35–57 in this book).[4] The Report was commissioned by the government of the day and followed a conference of working-class and educational organisations held at Oxford in the summer of 1907, entitled 'What Oxford Can Do For Working People'. The main issue discussed by the conference was the demand for higher education coming from working-class men and the role that the university might play in providing 'the education and culture many of them longed for'.[5] Albert Mansbridge was there, as leader of the recently established Workers Education Association (founded in 1903), taking the view that education was something spiritual and a means of individual enlightenment and self-fulfilment. At that time the WEA believed in academic impartiality and superiority, concepts which were anathema to some of those who had helped to establish Ruskin, 'for whom education which did not lead to political action, and eventually in a complete overthrow of the existing economy and society, was not only worthless, but traitorous to the cause.'[6]

The 1908 Report was produced by representatives of the University, the WEA and Ruskin College and resulted in the setting up of a joint committee of the university and of working people to be responsible for the conduct of tutorial classes outside the university.[7] Its concern was to take 'a broad reasoned view of things and a sane measure of social values'. Its purpose was to equip the working man [sic] with 'the civic qualities that enable him to co-operate with his fellows and to judge wisely on matters which concern not only himself, but the whole country to which he belongs', thus making him 'a more potent influence on the side of industrial peace.'[8] Values associated with social harmony rather than class struggle informed the report, providing little common ground with the Plebs League, established in the same year by Ruskin students to campaign for changes at the college who wanted 'nothing more nor less than the education of the workers in the interests of the workers'.[9]

In 1909 the Ruskin strike signified the dissatisfaction of Dennis Hird, the Ruskin Principal, and those students associated with the Plebs League, with attempts by the university to bring both the college and its curriculum more firmly under its control.[10] An intermittently recurring theme throughout Ruskin's history has been the contestation of views about education, in relation to the independence or incorporation of the working class, involving at times considerable tension between intellectual and political priorities, between different definitions of 'really useful knowledge', and about who exactly should be regarded as Ruskin's natural allies'.[11] The discussions which established Ruskin in the first place, which produced the 1908 Report and which led to the 1909 strike, can all be read as episodes in a continuing, internal debate, occasionally played out on a national stage, about the purpose and nature of education in relation to working-class people. This debate continues in the now fragmented, concealed and more complicated context of the present.

Harold Pollins, writing about the 1909 strike, suggests that

questions of politics, in relation to the proper purpose and auton
omy of working-class education, were less important than, th
personal antagonism within the small staff:

> Lees Smith, Buxton and Furniss were opposed to Hird, as the bitt
> comments in Furniss's autobiography document ... None of which
> intended to mean that the issue of independent working-class educ;
> tion was not a real one. But it does suggest that in differer
> circumstances and with different people the problems might have bee
> handled without an overt dispute.[12]

Hird's enforced resignation was upheld and Buxton, the vice prin
cipal, left at the end of 1909, somewhat disillusioned with Ruski
and with socialism, to fight the next election as a Liberal.

It could be that both views are right. The strike was indeed
notorious battle in the continuing struggle over purpose, alle
giance and definition; the Selbourne case was another.[13] Equall
small institutions which attract strong minded and idiosyncrati
individuals as tutors are capable of turf wars and 'principlec
disagreements that continue long after everyone has forgotten th
original point at issue. Pollins himself had a long-standing disput
with his fellow historian Raphael Samuel, both of whom wei
barely on speaking terms for most of their lengthy, joint membei
ship of a small group of twenty or so academic staff. Whil;
Samuel is widely credited with founding the History Worksho
Movement from his base at Ruskin, which by anybody's standarc
is recognised as being one of the important contributions to teacl
ing and writing about history in Britain in the period since th
1960s, Pollins's history of Ruskin, written in 1984, skips over th
achievement in two, rather grudging sentences.[14] Samuel was sim
larly ungenerous in his assessment of Pollins.

Those who learned their politics in the 1960s from the Ne
Left, as members of groups with socialist, Marxist, communi;
and Maoist tendencies, and who learned their academic stanc
from universities teaching critical social science and philosophy ;
about the same time, developed a questioning and adversarial vie
of the world which has contributed enormously to critical thinl
ing and critical intelligence. According to Jean Barr, it has also le

to an overly critical stance which can be a severe limitation and source of intellectual arrogance: 'the viewpoint of critical critique, ceaseless negation, carried out as if from nowhere, can itself become a kind of uncreative, dog-in-the-manger stubbornness which, in seeing value only in learning to criticise, has often little positive to say.'[15] The persistence, the lack of generosity, and the absolute certainty about some of this did not help the crisis of the left in the disarray that accompanied the Thatcher years,[16] and will not secure the future for Ruskin now, unless some dedicated, personal, political and epistemological lessons are learned from the residue of what is an overtly masculinist, rationalist and adversarial intellectual tradition.[17]

It is now accepted that historical writing is prone to the kind of revisionism that seeks to interpret the past in ways that reflect the preoccupations of the present[18], or which are coloured by sentiments deriving from nostalgia or romanticism – especially in autobiographical writing and especially about class.[19] In this context, it is worth commenting that Denis Hird and the Plebs League have become more celebrated for their radical stand in retrospect than was recognised at the time. College folklore has recast the strikers as the heroes of the piece, even though they did not win. Lord Bill McCarthy, speaking recently on Radio 4, was eager to set the record straight, arguing that, in trying to turn Ruskin into an openly socialist college, separate from the university, and a forcing house for revolution, 'Hird never got a majority. He never got a majority of the governing body. He never got a majority of the tutors. He never got a majority of the students. And in the end he went off and founded his own Central London Labour College ... which failed.'[20]

The socialist economist R.H.Tawney retained his commitment to the college, and made an occasional contribution to teaching, partly as a way of reforming Oxford University, but also because he had been influenced by earlier, radical definitions of 'really useful knowledge' which linked the purpose of education to social movements and social change. William Cobbett, for example, had wanted working-class people to understand and have better control over their own lives.[21] Robert Owen had taught working people that they had a right to learn who they were in relation to

past ages, and to the period in which they lived, and the circum
stances in which they were placed.[22]

In 1926 Tawney wrote:

> If I were asked what is the creative force which has carried forwar
> educational movements, I should reply: the rise of new classes, of nev
> forms of social structure, of new cultural and economic relationship:
> All these movements have regarded education not simply as an intere:
> or an ornament. They have regarded it as a dynamic, and there is noth
> ing at all surprising or regrettable in that. Knowledge has been sough
> in fact to meet a need. That need has been sometimes intellectual, it ha
> been sometimes religious, it has been social, it has been technical, bu
> the process ... is as much educational in the latter case as it is in the firs
> ... If you want flowers you must have flowers, roots and all, unless yo
> are satisfied, as many people are satisfied, with flowers made of pape
> and tinsel. And if you want education you must not cut it off from th
> social interests in which it has its living and perennial sources.[23]

This is surely an argument which is still relevant, in favour c
relating education to the material conditions of people's lives; t
people organising around their social and political interests; t
people in pursuit of social advancement and democratic participa
tion in democratic institutions and decision making arenas; it i
also an argument in favour of personal development; in whic
what counts as education is broadly defined and based o
dialogue, not simply the transmission of knowledge and skills. I
is, in other words, a view of education which involves a dialectica
and organic relationship with social movements.[24]

Over the years, trade unionists, left-wing political activists o
various kinds, pacifists, human rights activists, members of free
dom struggles from the third world, and more recently ecologist
feminists, homelessness and anti poverty campaigners, ethni
minorities, community and user groups, have all come to Ruski
as students seeking the 'really useful knowledge' that might hel
to advance the interests of progressive social and political move
ments. Some of their aspirations have been met, others have no
In the end it is rather random what you end up learning, and wh
teaches you. But if the radical spirit of Ruskin is to survive, it i

worth asking whether such commitments and connections could be less idiosyncratic and more systemic, more transparent and more coherent.

In 1909 those who favoured academic respectability in association with the university, and a less partisan approach to solidarity with the class struggle, as Bill McCarthy pointed out, won the day. The radicals lost. Ninety years later, times have changed. Allegiances are formed in different quarters. Definitions of what constitutes 'radical' are widely contested, not least because the term was appropriated by the New Right during the Thatcher years, in the execution of policies and ideas that considerably rearranged the existing political landscape. However, within the radical tradition in adult education – based on emancipatory learning linked to the struggle for progressive social change – its meaning lives on in debates about liberating knowledge, cultural diversity, popular education for democracy, learning through struggle, sustainable development, and feminism.[25] Were any of these to be debated openly in Ruskin today – as a way of agreeing on a re-visioned purpose for the future, which would then be embodied in the organisation, curriculum and culture of the college, to 'meet a need', as Tawney put it, and to work in dialogue and partnership with members of those educationally and socially dispossessed constituencies which Ruskin was established to serve – my guess is that the radicals would lose again. A public debate in Ruskin about the question 'What kind of education?' – in relation to lone parents and working-class women, for example, or unemployed workers, the residents of pauperised communities or survivors groups – would lead to fiercely contested disagreement about knowledge, purpose and allegiance. Those advocating a political and praxis oriented solidarity with adults marginalised by poverty and stigmatised by social pathologies would be defeated by a college culture unwilling to commit itself in practice to democratising education, or working for progressive social change beyond the rhetoric of academic discourse.

The fact that such a debate is not happening openly in the college, in any kind of exhilarating or sustained way that might then allow a radical and collectively articulated vision for the future to emerge, is perhaps some indication of an absence of radical energy. 'In a society in which learning is unequal, certain distinctive kinds of ignorance accumulate in the very heartland of learning. This heartland defines itself; it defines what learning is; it defines what is a subject and what is not. It knows what is evidence and what is not.'[26] The structure and content of the college curriculum would look very different in the centenary year if the structure of feelings and the resources for a journey of hope exemplified by the radical tradition in adult education, and personified in the Plebs' commitment to liberating knowledge from the control of the university and to class solidarity, had triumphed, rather than the elitism, and subsequent inertia, of the university connection.[27]

'Good' universities – as distinct from 'new' universities – have been added to Oxbridge over the years as jewels in the crown to which Ruskin students should aspire. But the voice of pragmatism also recognises that continuing funding will depend on diversification as distinct from elitism. The selection of a new Principal in 1998, to lead Ruskin into the millennium, would have been very different if the elitist tradition was still seen as a priority – or indeed if the college's somewhat unconsummated relationship with social and political radicalism was about to be re-visioned for the future. Instead the choice was made in favour of managerialism.

It remains to be seen what kind of survival this choice implies but the insistent questions that adult educators still need to be asked, and to ask themselves, are, as John Payne argues, 'Who benefits?' And 'In whose interests?'.[28] Neither managerialism nor academicism will do justice to the legacy of Ruskin's history, including the radical (often unfulfilled) desires that created the spirit and emotion of the centenary gala, still clamouring for recognition and still, I would suggest, a source of energy to be built upon, if the will to do so still exists. However, history alone does not fully explain the contradictory character of choices being made in the present. Neither can it solve the problems of the future. But its lessons can help us to imagine what future possibilities might exist.

In 1997, just six months after another Labour landslide, the National Advisory Group for Continuing Education and Lifelong

Learning (NAGCELL) presented its first report to government in anticipation of new legislation concerning adult and continuing education. Ruskin was not invited to be part of this group, although the return of a Labour government, and an education minister with some knowledge of the radical tradition in adult education and close links with residential colleges, was some solace to adult educators with very different priorities to those pursued by the Tories. Back onto the agenda came ideas about the politics, purpose and philosophy of adult education as distinct from technical, quantative and institutional modifications to systems and organisations. The aspirations were forward looking but the debates were not exactly new. They involved widening participation in further and higher education and establishing the right of the many, rather than the few, to lifelong learning opportunities and recognised qualifications. They drew attention to the condition of impoverished communities as ghettos for the poor in which community and outreach education could have a vital role to play in community regeneration and democratic participation. They demanded more ambitious plans for working with voluntary organisations and trade unions to make sure that vocational and workplace learning are about something more educational than behaviourism and skills training.

The group chairman was Bob Fryer, then Principal of Northern College. His deputy was Alan Tuckett, Director of the National Institute of Adult Continuing Education. Other prominent voices, with experience of working-class, trade union and residential college education, included John Field, now Professor of Lifelong Learning at the University of Warwick, Keith Jackson, then Principal of Fircroft College, and Jim Sutherland, Head of the Education Department at Unison.

Ruskin's active involvement could have been viewed as superfluous, given the leadership of Fryer and the role played by Jackson and Sutherland in co-ordinating subgroups on community and citizenship and workplace learning. But Ruskin's absence from the line-up, with a membership invigorated by the reawakening of possibilities and opportunities brought about by the change of government, in which enlightened and socially committed voices occupied influential roles, speaks volumes about the ways in which the College was viewed by those who drew up the terms of reference and appointed the participants.

The first report of NAGCELL is not the most radical of documents – as might be expected from a group that wants to effect and influence what actually happens, rather than analyse and be critical about what does not. But it does demonstrate considerable concern about the personal and social consequences to individuals and communities of continuing educational exclusion, in ways that are not simply determined by society's needs and the state's ongoing preoccupation with economic competitiveness and social cohesion. And it is committed to provision that takes seriously the political and social context of education.[29]

Ruskin's absence should not be regarded as a comment on the extent or otherwise of the radicalness involved in persuading government to 'try harder' in relation to social justice and educational advancement. Rather it is an indictment of the college's lack of standing in wider public debates about education and social change. The 'arrogance' and 'lack of generosity' that Barr referred to as a legacy of critical social science in the 1960s is also a function of extreme defensiveness and lack of confidence. Institutions that are enthusiastic and strongly committed to what they are doing, and which have the confidence that comes from public recognition, as well as from knowing they are doing a good job, can afford to let the evidence speak for itself and can be generous towards others with whom they share a common interest.[30] This would include active participation in the political and educational debates of the day. Of course, Ruskin might still survive, whilst failing to be so engaged. But not, it seems, from a position of prominence and credibility concerning the interests of working-class and educationally disadvantaged constituencies, or in collaboration with others in adult education and the labour movement who think that trying to influence these debates is important.

Class solidarity and the class struggle are no longer the allegiances that are being promoted in Tony Blair's New Britain, but neither are they concepts which carry much weight in Ruskin. It is true to say that the majority of students at Ruskin still come from working-class and lower working-class backgrounds, with few or no previous qualifications. In the centenary year, for example, 53 per cent of those on the Certificate in Higher Education Programme (equivalent to the first year of undergraduate study) were unwaged on entry; 39 per cent were women; 15 per cent were from ethnic minority backgrounds; 68 per cent had GCSE or no qualifications. No one addressing the assembled student body on the first day of the academic year, as I did, would be in any doubt about where they were coming from in a social class sense. But on Sunday 29 November 1998 the *Observer* announced, 'It's Official. We're all middle-class now'. What the newspaper was referring to was the introduction of a new, eight-tier table of social classifications, based on occupations, unveiled by the National Statistical Office, most of which were defined as middle-class. Being working-class, it seems, was no longer very relevant. The news passed without much notice or comment in a college dedicated, by its founders, to the education of working-class people. Perhaps not surprisingly.

It is almost a decade now since John Major promised to deliver a classless society.[31] This was not to be a society without classes but a society providing the means for people to advance by ability, regardless of their class origins. It was to be 'an opportunity society' in which the role of government was to 'provide the ladders' enabling citizens to rise to 'whatever level their own abilities and good fortune may take them from whatever their starting point' (*Times* 25.7.90). In fact, Major's classless society was little more than the well worn commitment to meritocracy, based on the illusion of mobility for those with ambition and ability from low class backgrounds. Its focus was on the individual rather than the collective. But, as Adonis and Pollard argue:

> the condition of classes is far more important than the mobility between them. Minorities are on the ladder; majorities stay put ... the capacity of individuals to climb at all depends upon them not being more than a ladder length from their destination. And there is always downward mobility ... the further the fall, the greater the grievance and despair ... for all its drawbacks, the word Underclass captures the essence of the class predicament for many at the bottom: a complete absence of ladders, whether basic skills, role models, education or a culture of work.[32]

Margaret Thatcher's notorious view of society was that 'there is no such thing', and her view on class was 'the least said about it the better' – on the basis that the more you talk about something, the more you give the idea credibility in people's minds. Margaret Thatcher said a few odd things in her time but this was probably one of her more perceptive remarks, although not mentioning class has not made it go away. Widening educational participation will not solve class oppression. Individual solutions do not solve the problems of class relations in capitalism. You can't get rid of class conflict (or sexual oppression or racism) with therapy. Conditions of structural inequality have not disappeared despite the view in post modern Britain that class is an inaccurate term, unless like 'race' and 'woman' it is placed between inverted commas. But the discussion about it has been dying, politically and academically, for the best part of twenty years. And it is the working class who have lost.

The outcome of the class war was not decided simply by the defeat of the miners, but the battle for the Yorkshire coalfield was a defining moment. The twin traits of Thatcherism – ruthlessness and individualism – finally managed to make the working class no longer dangerous. They were bullied and incorporated, turned into an underclass and silenced. New Labour does not speak for them. It speaks for those John Prescott calls 'the beautiful people', and for the professional classes whose autonomy and professionalism were attacked by Thatcher. The old Labour solution to poverty and structural inequalities, based on upping the taxation of the better off, to increase spending on the badly off, whilst strengthening the role of the state to mop up unemployment, is most definitely not the political platform that won Labour the 1997 election. Blair's version of a stakeholder society, a third way, a New Britain, is to persuade more people to think of themselves as middle-class. Speaking in 1996, he said, 'our task is to allow more people to become middle-class. The Labour party did not come into being to celebrate working-class people having a lack of opportunity and poverty, but to take them out of it' (*Sunday Times* 1.9.96). Since at least the 1980s, the choice on offer to the working class, whatever political party has been in power, has been to get on their bikes, retrain, move from welfare into work and pin their faith in Education. Education. Education. New Labour's New Deal – put like this – is pretty straightforward: strive to join the middle class or rot in the badlands of the under-class.

The 'amazing disappearance of the working class' works quite well as a theory if you have a full time job yourself and feel enthusiastic about Labour's third way. It is convincing – just about – if you take the view that the chronological passage of time equals social progress, and if you do not risk testing your hypothesis in the real world – in those areas where manufacturing and heavy industry have disappeared, especially in the North, in Central Scotland, South Wales, Northern Ireland and large parts of the Midlands, where hospital cleaners, factory workers, shop assistants and building workers go about their daily business; where housing has never been more polarised, and where housing tenure is now, more than ever, an accurate predictor of health, income, educational level, alcohol and drug abuse, and the likelihood of unemployment. And from where Ruskin students still come, looking for a way to change their lives.

Of course, Ruskin tutors know this intellectually, but for the most part respond in terms of academic and individualist notions of education, as a way of helping individuals to climb out from under, an imagined solution which is somewhat undermined by the absence of any consistent correlation between being working-class, acquiring a qualification and securing social and economic advancement.[33] This solution also relies on the ladder view of education in which the ladder is narrow rather than wide, providing individual rather than collective mobility. It ignores the fact that many of those who scramble up go off and play for the other side, that some have little chance of starting the climb at all, and that many who try, fail.[34] It is a response that lacks a late modern analysis of class, and which no longer implies a praxis oriented view of collective solidarity with working-class people and their various, related struggles. It is generally more nostalgic about what was, and complacent about what is, than imaginative about what might be.

In Ruskin folklore, the National Union of Mineworkers and Wapping are emblematic of a heroic past, associated with noble intentions and socialist dreams in which all the heroes were white men and all the women were wives. This is a view of history which was seriously challenged by the energy of the women's choir, singing songs at the centenary celebrations about women's strikes, Greenham Common and the Women Against Pit Closures campaign, beneath banners celebrating black and white women's activism in trade unions, the peace movement and feminist campaigns against male violence. The heroic past was a time in Ruskin when George Orwell and D.H. Lawrence dominated the English Studies curriculum, when men were seen as agents of socialist history, when more complex relationships with the world were not allowed, and women scarcely appeared at all. It was a time when Labour Studies was seen as central to an understanding of affiliation and political struggle, in ways that paid little or no attention to women's concerns in the labour market and no attention at all to issues of re-production and domestic labour relations. These are concerns still missing from Labour Studies teaching in the college. In reviewing the frequent sexism and conservatism of socialist and working-class politics, Beatrix Campbell asks, 'what would make us think that trade union involvement is any different from anything else? It's only another place where men and women live out their conflict of interests. It's only another site of struggle in which women have been defeated by what feminist labour historian Barbara Taylor calls men's 'sexual Toryism'.[35]

The first national Women's Liberation Movement conference took place at Ruskin in 1970 but is not mentioned in the college's official history, although it is extremely important in the history of second wave feminism.[36] Sally Alexander, a student at the time, describes aggressive men 'enraged at their college being taken over by all these women, all these children, at the mess, at the disruption, at the slogans being painted ... They couldn't go into the television room and watch sport ... The complaints about the television room and the mess were a cover for something which seemed really disruptive and threatening.[37]

Women's Studies did not appear in the college curriculum until 1993 and it took appointments of women at about the same period in sociology and history before any serious consideration of women's lives in studies of society, cultural politics and history took place. Of course, feminist commentators such as Beatrix Campbell and Carolyn Steedman have done much to draw attention to absences and silences about women's experiences.[38] Their work examines the lives of working-class people in communities in a way that recognises, but does not romanticise, working-class masculinity, which identifies conflicts and contradictions in class and gender politics, and which pays attention to working-class women's lived experience as something very different from that of working-class men's, in ways that can no longer be subsumed conceptually within masculinist generalisations or traditional class analysis.

It is hardly surprising that students coming to Ruskin from working-class backgrounds at the end of the 1990s are less likely, than in previous times to articulate a strong sense of class identity – or pride – however masculinist that version of reality might have been. The opportunities for developing class solidarity in working-class organisations and communities of mutual interest have suffered from 'the death of politics' during the Conservative years. Parliamentary politics have ceased to engage with social meanings and lived experience outside the concerns of corporate party interests; people are disenfranchised in much the same way as Chomsky shows for large sections of the lower class, black and recent immigrant groups in the United States – the system pays no attention to their concerns, and then defines them as apathetic for showing no interest in the democratic process.[39]

The present House of Commons is more uniform in appearance – socially and ideologically – than any since the Great Reform Act of 1832. The arrival of Labour women in significant numbers in 1997 helped to shift the gender balance but did nothing to alter the fact that more than four fifths of today's MPs have professional, executive or managerial backgrounds. If the old aristocracy has mostly disappeared from the Tory side, so too have Labour's authentic working-class trade unionists – down to 1 in 5 of all Labour MPs by 1996. Parliamentary politics has become an all consuming career; an increasing number of its practitioners have made it into something very different at the end of the century from what it was at the beginning. As Adonis and Pollard argue, the professionalisation of politics had discouraged the non careerists from taking part'.[40] Not only has the practice of parliamentary politics become less accessible to ordinary people, the perception on the part of growing numbers of citizens is that they cannot influence what politicians do. Both parties advocate a classless 'one nation' society and swap identical buzzwords to do with choice, freedom, individuality and opportunity. In the meantime, 'Acute social segregation and the lack of aspiration among the lower classes co-exist with a pervasive sense of political impotence and it is hard to believe that the two are unconnected'.[41]

Organised working-class politics, expressed through local government action and trade unions, have suffered from a reduction in their power and incorporation, from punitive and repressive legislation, the disciplining and demoralising effects of unemployment and increasing poverty, privatisation and deregulation. Middle-class intellectuals and academics – of the kind employed at Ruskin – who were involved in socialist and feminist politics in the 1960s and 1970s, are likely to have lost some of their momentum in the 1990s, brought on by the crisis in the left and the backlash against feminism. Individuals who have been overcome by cultural pessimism or cannot get enthusiastic about the future of radical politics have increasingly turned to personal solutions to occupy their energies, or they have given up. Whilst teachers make up the single largest occupational group among the membership of both political parties, 'politicians of all hues and ... many educators demonstrate little interest in deepening the quality of life, in extending democracy through enlarging our capacities for thinking, criticising, creating and controlling'.[42]

Hope lies, as ever, in the resilience of those on the front line – especially women, whom Beatrix Campbell calls 'the true radicals' – in creative anger, disaffection, oppositional culture, and the will to resist that which is manifestly unjust.[43] It helps, of course, to be organised rather than idiosyncratic, and collectivist rather than individualist, if social change is the desired objective. Far more people currently belong to self-help groups, community organisations and social movements than are members of political parties. Their political potential comes from the creation of space for participation and dialogue in relation to issues with which they are concerned. According to Anthony Giddens, 'they can force into the discursive domain aspects of social conduct that previously went undiscussed, or were "settled" by traditional practices. They may help contest "official" definitions of things; feminist, ecological, and peace movements have all achieved this outcome, as have a multiplicity of self help groups'.[44] This kind of sub politics is evident in Ruskin in the irreverence and energy of working-class women; among working-class men who are actively involved in renegotiating a more egalitarian and democratic settlement with women; and in the courage of those who survive racism, abuse, the degradation of poverty and unemployment, and who get on with their lives despite enormous odds.

If Ruskin is to survive, it needs to articulate a strong response to shifting political and educational landscapes and to rejuvenate its philosophic base as a commitment to future intent and purpose.

It is worth asking what a culture of generosity would look like as the basis for more positive and collective energy, which could be spent in developing the kind of vision that radical educationalists could happily endorse. What sorts of changes in college culture and consciousness are worth pursuing in the interests of regenerating solidarities, and of building connections and organisational strategies through dialogue rather than managerialism? Could Ruskin be transformed into the kind of organisation in which learning is about more effective collaboration, about valuing diversity, about building a democratic and tolerant culture, about dialogue and reflexive communication?

In curriculum terms this would include finding better ways of engaging with the learning needs of working-class people, whose previous experiences of education have often been alienating and defeating. Ruskin should take pride in not contributing a single lesson to the store of humiliations or failures from previous educational defeats. This approach would include a challenging and rigorous attitude to what counts as knowledge, and making the quality and comprehensive range of students' learning a priority. For all of us 'the need to know' is enormous in a world which is changing rapidly, in which the gap between the well educated and the badly educated is increasing, and in which people's capacity to shape the changes taking place must include all citizens in the process of development and change.

Educational provision should stem from the concerns and conditions of prospective Ruskin students, from the constituencies they represent, which Ruskin was established to serve. It should not stem from the professional self interest of academics, or from a managerialist interest in the commodification and delivery of courses as a function of funding separate from an educational, committed, dialectical and organic relationship with social movements. This would mean a mixture of provision – in relation to content, levels, structure, duration and delivery systems. It would mean the expansion of outreach activities, a big investment in IT, more recognition of students' lifelong learning needs and priorities, and more attention to student diversity, to knowledge that is useful to those who are activists and participants in social change. It would mean the principled pursuit of collaboration, and connection and commitment to the distinctive educational, social and political advancement of hitherto marginalised and excluded groups within the working class. And it would require the imagination, flexibility and intellectual energy of all those involved, to turn the principles into practice.

Words like solidarity, commitment, collaboration, transformation, liberation and allegiance should properly be reclaimed, as a declaration of intention to make educational provision that is 'roots and all' and 'not cut off from the social interests in which it has its living and perennial sources' into a reality.[45] As well as looking backwards to its roots in radical (and unfulfilled) desires, and inwards to the quality and character of its educational provision and its culture, Ruskin must increasingly look outwards – to its place in the wider world, and to the contribution it might make to the educational and political discussions of the day. It should begin to work towards helping to shape what happens in the interests of working-class people, and to put academic theories – about challenging social exclusion and increasing democratic participation – into practice.[46] This must include greater recognition of the issues facing women and black and ethnic minorities, for whom the existence of racism, of partisan deals done in 'smoke filled rooms', and of men's 'sexual Toryism' have not disappeared; it needs to be recognised that Ruskin remains an organisation that also has its roots in the white working class and the liberal academic 'men's movement'.[47]

Far from being solved, the continuing inequalities deriving from structural divisions associated with social class, ethnicity and gender still require something more from Ruskin tutors than weekly essays and tutorials, masculinist assumptions about the heroic past, and precious little analysis about constructions of race\gender\class identity in the present. If Ruskin is to do better than survive, it needs to take a decision to make a major contribution to the future of radical politics in a way which democratises education and relates it the kinds of 'really useful knowledge' which will enable individuals and groups to make things happen, rather than have things happen to them. The future agenda for radicals in adult education must be to work together with those who have a material and political interest in progressive social change, and for whom liberating knowledge and increased control over their own lives is the benchmark for a more participatory and actively democratic society.

My thanks to Sylvia Vance for her insightful comments on the initial draft of this chapter.

NOTES

1. Harold Pollins, *The History of Ruskin College*, Ruskin College Library, Occasional Publication 3, Oxford 1984, p9.
2. Hilda Kean, 'Myths of Ruskin College' in *Studies in Adult Education*, Vol 20, No 2, 1996.
3. James Callaghan, in *Centenary Gala Programme*, Ruskin College, Oxford, 20 February 1999.
4. *Oxford and Working Class Education*,1908; *The Final Report of the Adult Education Committee of the Ministry of Reconstruction*, 1919; *The Ashby Report*, 1954; *The Russell Report*, 1973; *Learning For The Twenty First Century: Report of the National Advisory Group for Continuing Education and Lifelong Learning*, 1997.
5. Sylvia Harrop (ed), *Oxford and Working Class Education: A New*

Introduction to the 1908 Report, Continuing Education Press, Universit of Nottingham 1987, p2.

6. *Ibid.*.
7. Pollins 1984, *op.cit.*.
8. *Oxford and Working Class Education*,1908 Report, paragraph 82, see no 4; paragraph 139.
9. Editorial in *Plebs*, 1:1, February 1909, p4.
10. Roger Fieldhouse, 'The 1908 Report: Antidote to Class Struggle?', in th volume.
11. Richard Johnson, '"Really Useful Knowledge": Radical Education an Working Class Culture', in Clarke, Critcher and Johnson (eds), *Workir Class Culture*, Hutchinson 1979.
12. Pollins 1984, *op.cit.*.
13. Geoff Andrews, 'Left apart: Raphael Samuel, David Selbourne and th crisis of the Left in the 1980s', in this volume .
14. Pollins 1984, *op.cit.*, pp53-54 .
15. Jean Barr, *Liberating Knowledge: Research, Feminism and Adu Education*, NIACE 1999.
16. Geoff Andrews, see note 13.
17. Jane Thompson, *Out From Under: Women, Class and Educatio* Routledge, London, forthcoming.
18. Sylvia Vance, 'Lorca's Mantle: The Rise of Fascism and the Work of Stor Jameson', in *Women Writers of the 1930s: Gender, Politics and Histor* Maroula Joannou (ed), Edinburgh University Press, Edinburgh 1999.
19. John Burnett (ed), *Useful Toil: Autobiographies of Working People fro the 1820s to the 1920s*, Allen Lane 1974; Hilda Kean, 'Radical Adu Education: The Reader and the Self', in Marjorie Mayo and Ja Thompson (ed), *Adult Learning, Critical Intelligence and Social Chang* National Institute of Adult and Continuing Education, Leicester 199 David Vincent (ed), *Testaments of Radicalism: Memoirs of Working Cla Politicians 1790-1885*, Europa Publications 1977.
20 Lord Bill McCarthy, *Ruskin at a Hundred*, BBC Radio Four, 11 Mar 1999.
21. Raymond Williams, 'Adult Education and Social Change: Lectures ar Reminiscences in Honour of Tony McLean', *Border Country: Raymor Williams in Adult Education*, John McIlroy and Sallie Westwood (ed National Institute of Adult Continuing Education, Leicester 1993, p258
22. Harold Silver, *The Concept of Popular Education*, McGibbon and Kee 196
23. R.H.Tawney, 'Adult Education in the History of the Nation', paper re at the fifth Annual Conference of the British Institute of Adult Educatio 1926, pp20, 22.

24. Keith Jackson, 'Popular Education and the State: A New Look at the Community Debate', *Adult Learning, Critical Intelligence and Social Change*, Marjorie Mayo and Jane Thompson (eds), NIACE, Leicester 1995, p184.

25. On liberating knowledge see Jean Barr 1999, *op.cit.*; on cultural diversity see Rebecca O'Rourke, 'All Equal Now?', in Mayo and Thompson, *op.cit.* and Mary Stuart and Alistair Thomson (eds), *Engaging With Difference: the 'Other' in Adult Education*, NIACE 1995; on popular education for democracy see Jim Crowther, Ian Martin and Mae Shaw (eds), *Popular Education and Social Movements in Scotland Today*, NIACE, Leicester 1998; on learning through struggle see Griff Foley, *Learning in Social Action: A Contribution to Understanding Informal Education*, Zed Books 1999; on sustainable development see Marjorie Mayo, *Imagining Tomorrow: Adult Education for Transformation*, NIACE 1997; and on feminism see Jane Thompson, *Words in Edgeways: Radical Learning For Social Change*, NIACE, 1997.

26. Williams, 'Adult Education and Social Change', in WEA South Eastern District, *Adult Education and Social Change: Lectures and Reminiscences in Honour of Tony McClean*, 1983.

27. Williams, *Politics and Letters*, NLB/Verso 1979; Williams, *Resources of Hope*, Verso 1989.

28. John Payne, 'Adult Learning in the Context of Global, Neo Liberal Economic Policies', in Mayo and Thompson, *op.cit.*.

29. *Learning For The Twenty First Century*, 1997 Report, see note 4.

30. I am grateful for the elucidation of this insight to my colleague at Ruskin, Ann Schofield.

31. At a press conference 20/11/90.

32. Andrew Adonis and Stephen Pollard, *A Class Act: The Myth of Britain's Classless Society*, Penguin Books 1997, pp15-16.

33. Thompson, forthcoming, see note 17.

34. Williams, 'Figures and Shadows' in *The Highway*, February 1954, pp169-72.

35. Beatrix Campbell, *Wigan Pier Revisited: Poverty and Politics in the 1980s*, Virago, London 1984.

36. Anna Coote and Beatrix Campbell, *Sweet Freedom*, Blackwell, Oxford, second edition 1987.

37. Sally Alexander, 'Interview', in Micheline Wandor (ed), *Once a Feminist: Stories of a Generation*, Virago, London 1990, pp88-89.

38. Beatrix Campbell 1984, *op.cit.*, and *Goliath: Britain's Dangerous Places*, Methuen 1993; Carolyn Steedman, *Landscape for a Good Woman*, Virago, London 1986.

39. Noam Chomsky, *Chronicles of Dissent: Interviews with David Barsamian*, Common Courage Press, Maine 1992.
40. Adonis and Pollard 1997, *op.cit.*, p129.
41. *Ibid.*, p130.
42. John McIlroy, in McIlroy and Westwood (ed), 1993, *op.cit.*, p18.
43. Campbell 1984, *op.cit.*.
44. Anthony Giddens, *Beyond Right and Left: The Future of Radical Politics*, Polity Press, Cambridge 1994.
45. R.H.Tawney 1926, *op.cit.*.
46. Steedman 1986, *op.cit.*.
47. Campbell 1984, *op.cit.*.

Look, see, hear: A remembrance, with approaches to contemporary public history at Ruskin

PAUL MARTIN

RAPPING ON RAPH

No account of history at Ruskin in its centenary year can begin without referring to Raphael Samuel, who in many ways defined the current Ruskin approach to history. Being the self-effacing man that he was, usually preferring to hear and talk about what others were doing rather than talking about himself, he would no doubt blanch at this idea. However, as an ex-history student (1986-88) and since 1997 a history lecturer at Ruskin, and one of many who benefited from his approach to history, I feel it appropriate to offer a remembrance in terms of my own experience at Ruskin during Raph's time there.

I entered Ruskin as a history student, with a passion for labour history, having been a shop steward on a government work scheme. I came, like many others, with a ready-made indifference to the 'top end' of history, and an unquenchable thirst after what 'ordinary people' did in the past. Only after my first sessions with Raph did I discover that this was what other people called social history! My writing skills were perfunctory at the time to say the least, and as my early essays floundered for want of structure, Raph would gently advise: 'Comrade, you must think like a lawyer, you are arguing a case on behalf of your client'. This in itself seemed to help. Now rereading my first term report from Raph, his generosity of spirit comes clearly through: 'Paul has a

---

vast knowledge of the byways of history and a splendid ability to use original quotations and sources. He writes with great vigour.' This was his way of sweetening the fact that I went into great depth on detail only peripherally related to the essay subject, asserting it as though it were the central point! Raph gave the first lecture I attended at Ruskin's Headington site. I believe the lecture was on new unionism in the 1890s. I remember three things about this initial lecture. Firstly, on hearing him talk about labour history, I immediately felt 'safe' at Ruskin (a feeling other students have also expressed); I had made the right decision to come. Raph was the first person in any authority I had encountered to whom I immediately ideologically related, or who I felt thought like me. Secondly, I remember him asserting that unions for uniformed workers (e.g. tram workers, postmen etc.) in the late nineteenth century were very few, at which point I made a knee-jerk interjection and blurted out a list of such unions, and at such a pace that he could not write them down quickly enough! He was kind enough afterwards to thank me for the information of which he had been unaware. This was probably my first encounter with his educational credo of interactive learning. My third memory of that lecture relates to his endearing eccentricity. He was chalking notes on the continuous chalk board and ran out of room at the bottom end; and rather than pull the surface down, to reach the blank part above, he walked the length of the lecture hall and got a chair on which he stood in order to use the top of the board. Only when a student rather timidly advised him that he could pull the surface downwards did he realise! This was perhaps also the only time I can remember Raph giving a lecture to students in the conventional sense; thereafter he reverted to his preferred mode of the seminar in a smaller room. I always preferred this arrangement as a student and still prefer it as a lecturer. Affording as it does a more interactive environment, it positions the lecturer as moderator rather than a mere talking head. It encourages students to share with and learn from each other, rather than look to the lecturer as the sole arbiter of knowledge. Thus it was the perfect form for someone with a democratic approach to education.

My project at the end of my two years, I decided, was to be on the history and use of the lapel badge in the trade union movement over a one hundred year period.[1] I received reactions varying from wry smiles and quizzical looks to outright laughter from those to whom I mentioned the project; Raph was the only one who accepted it at face value, as though its validity and interest were self evident. As my supervisor he was never less than enthusiastic and supportive. At a history workshop convention not long afterwards in Brighton, I gave my first public presentation, at Raph's invitation.

The story of History Workshop, the movement and the journal, is related elsewhere.[2] It is sufficient to say, and without exaggeration, that its effect was to revolutionise approaches to history in Britain. It built on, and indeed epitomised, 'history from below', imbued as it was with the optimism of the 1960s. What it also gave was a mutual platform and audience for popular dissent, and an arena in which the story of people's lives and experience was given historical validity. As Sheila Rowbotham recounted: ' ... what the History Workshop opened up was the personal perspective, the sort of experiential stuff which was around in some of that late 1960s writing in general about politics: it introduced the actual experience of education'.[3] Hitherto, ordinary people had largely been the *object* of study, in the context of organisations (such as trade unions and co-ops); now their voices were to be heard as historically valid in their own right.

Raphael Samuel's and the History Workshop legacy at Ruskin is a vibrant tradition of historical argument and analysis. It is also a legacy of a very honourable and healthy disrespect for academic pomposity. History at Ruskin, I am glad to say, continues in this tradition! Raph's philosophy was that anything and everything we encountered in life on an everyday basis had the potential to tell us something about history or culture. As the *History Workshop Journal* (HWJ) collective editorial for its first issue stated: 'We believe that history is a source of inspiration and understanding, furnishing not only the means of interpreting the past but also the best critical vantage point from which to view the present'.[4] It is within this ethos that much of the teaching on Ruskin's MA in Public History and Popular Memory, and the Certificate in Higher Education (CHE), is conducted. The MA was, sadly, Raph's last Ruskin initiative, but it was one which was intended to take his concept of history into the twenty-first century. The first HWJ editorial in 1976 stated that: ' ... we believe that history should become a common property, capable of shaping people's understanding of themselves and the society in which they live.'[5] The 1980s and 1990s have been a period of radical change in which many people have felt themselves alienated from society. But Public History at Ruskin reasserts the HWJ's belief, by addressing ways in which people can reposition themselves in a changing society and reclaim empowerment by embracing different forms of expression of selfhood in a historical context. These can take many forms including material and visual culture, oral and aural and literary forms. It is 'public history' because it embraces and values knowledge gained, ideas formed and sources used from outside of the academy. It is, as was always intended, a development in democratic scholarship.[6]

SEEING IS BELIEVING: THE EVERYDAY ENCOUNTER

It was Raph's intention to draw on 'texts' other than the written word for the MA (aural, oral and visual) and it is an approach that Hilda Kean and I, who teach the MA, have pursued with relish. What follows are snapshots of some themes I have covered during the visual culture (second) term of the MA. They are illustrative of approaches to contemporary history from the standpoint of everyday encounter. As Raph wrote: 'A history that was alert to its constituency would need to address not only the record of the past but also the hidden forces shaping contemporary understandings of it, the imaginative complexes in and through which it is perceived'.[7] In furtherance of this objective, I have chosen to offer the example of material culture, beginning with rubbish! This is employed to show how people use it to create meaning. This then leads into a discussion on contemporary collecting and its motivations, which provides us with another perspective on history from below, that is history from objects. 'Read' in the context of their production and consumption, objects from Reform Act mugs to Spitting Image puppets, from Victorian crested china to *Beany Babies*, afford us some insight into the mentalities, in the *Annales* sense, of the last two centuries. In addition, as an example of how the aural has become important, popular music forms part of the first introductory term, which goes under the heading 'Public History Now'. By these means students themselves are encouraged to reflect on how they figure in the equation, and how their own histories are also part of a greater whole. This, I feel, is very much in keeping with the idea of democratic history as championed by Raph and History Workshop. This approach also involves looking at how we see ourselves, as Raph noted: 'If history is an arena for the projection of ideal selves, it can also be a means of undoing and questioning them, offering more disturbing accounts of who we are and where we come from than simple identification would suggest'.[8] This is what Public History at Ruskin is seeking to further the study of.

A LOAD OF OLD RUBBISH?

Material culture is one way in which individuals seek to project themselves. Its basest form, rubbish, can be used as a text from which to deduce this. Some people find meaning in what others would designate as rubbish. In so doing, they are often making visual statements about their own values or sense of self-worth. One way in which people have sought to make public statements about themselves has been by the construction of monuments or edifices made from discarded material and found objects. Most famously, the Watts Tower in Los Angeles, the work of Sabato (Sam) Rodia (1894-1965), an Italian immigrant, was constructed from steel and wire mesh, over a period of 34 years. It was:

> ... covered with 40,000 ornaments including pottery, glazed tiles, blue and green bottles, sea shells and rocks which he salvaged from around the neighbourhood. By the time the towers were finished in 1955, Rodia had built 17 sculptures, three tall spires, the largest nearly 100 feet high, two walls, a gazebo, several smaller towers, a ship and a patio. He called it Nuestro Pueblo, or Our Town, but it became known

as Watts Towers. He never told anyone his exact motivation. The only thing we know for sure is that throughout his life he constantly said 'I'm gonna do something, I'm gonna do something'.[9]

Other examples of this tendency include collage. Most famous perhaps in this context was Kurt Shwitters. Shwitters (1887-1948) produced some two thousand collages between 1918 and 1948.[10] He called his collages 'Mertz', derived from a cropped letterhead, which he found in the street, of the Komertz und Privat Bank in Hannover. He used tram tickets, cigarette packets, serviettes, cloakroom tickets, playing cards, envelopes, receipts, blotters and parcel paper to make his collages. He wrote that:

> Out of frugality, I drew on what came to hand, for we were a poverty stricken country [Germany after WW1]. One can still cry out by way of bits of rubbish and that is what I did, by gluing or nailing them together. This I called Mertz ... Nothing was left intact anyway and the thing was to build something new out of the broken past. [11]

Shwitters was using discarded materials, perhaps to express the way that he himself or people more generally felt discarded by the economic situation after WW1. It was the example of Shwitters that was partly responsible for one student's decision to reinterpret her accumulations of personal momentoes and pin boards of photographs etc. as something more meaningful. Combined with a museum trip (see below), this has led to some interesting writing and a high degree of self-revelation, through re-codifying what she had hitherto seen as sentimental clutter into a meaningful discourse on selfhood and the creation of meaning.

In wider, and institutional, terms, museums have been formed based on collections of rubbish. One such museum is 'Rejectamenta', run by Stella Mitchell in East Wittering, Sussex. This includes such exhibits as: '... a collage of sweet wrappers left by GIs during the second world war.'[12] As a child Mitchell would dig in ploughed fields, 'not for gold coins, but for pieces of broken crockery – green blue and brown willow pattern which she was sure would one day make up a whole plate...'[13] She was once known as 'Mrs Magpie'. More famously, Robert Opie's museum

'The Pack-Age', housed in a former warehouse in the Gloucester docks, boasts hundreds of thousands of labels, containers and advertising materials from the last 150 years. All of these are demonstrative of sources used in public history at Ruskin, and they are evidence of the validity of the encounters of the everyday that Raph was so passionate about.[14] There is also evidence for an increasing academic validation of such material elsewhere. In 1993 'The Centre for Ephemera Studies' was opened at the University of Reading. This is based on the 25 year long collection of transient material (from baked bean labels to prostitutes' cards left in telephone boxes) by the author and founder of the Ephemera Society, Maurice Rickards, who explained: 'Half of history appears on the library shelf, the other half in the waste paper basket'.[15] Raph would I am sure have supported its recovery! Leading from the decorative or other use of rubbish comes the more formalised activity of collecting, in which people are more knowingly engaged.

VICTORIAN VALUES

Collecting, although a personal activity in terms of the creation of meaning, is a very public act, carried out at car-boot sales and specialist fairs every week. Its popular (as opposed to classical) roots are based in the facilitation of mass production in the nineteenth century. The development of the 'train excursion' and the 'day trip' in the third quarter of the nineteenth century brought popular seaside and other destinations within the reach of the working class. As Blackpool, Skegness and other areas became defined by their working-class visitors, or 'trippers' as they were known, so a cheap souvenir industry grew up. By Edwardian times, postcards, imitation jet jewellery, crested china ornaments and other trinkets were available *en masse* in every seaside town where workers came to play. This was perhaps the real beginnings of popular collecting as we know it today.[16] There is an essentially uninvestigated history of popular collecting, which has so far managed to evade recent interest in leisure history. It has only become prominent on a populist basis (in Britain at least) over the last two decades. It is the kind of people's history that History Workshop delighted in revealing.

I COLLECT, THEREFORE I AM

Collecting itself is self-educational. It comprises one material cultural form in which public history is defined, forms which Raph was becoming increasingly interested in.[17] An example of extra-mural historical study is embraced in metal detecting: 'The collecting and study of metal items made and used by our fore-bears is a cerebral activity enjoyed by thousands who may not all have found equivalent interest during early education'.[18] As an aspect of lifelong learning, this has much to commend it. It also typifies the kind of experience Ruskin students may have, and which they would be encouraged to reappraise as a form of self assessment of prior learning. Popular collecting more broadly is in some ways complementary to family history, in that they are both concerned with finding personal fixity in an uncertain present, through reference to the past.[19] Popular collecting often finds expression as an extension of the self, in that the collector seeks to extend their psychological or moral self into the material world through the creation of the collection.[20] I have argued elsewhere that the burgeoning of popular collecting since the 1980s has been fuelled by the drastic cultural and socio-economic change in society over this period, in which people subliminally seek sanctuary from the pace or extent of such change through the collection of motifs or symbols of security, or objects which seem to define values or ways of being that are perceived to be in decline in society at large.[21] On the MA in Public History, such propositions are put and explored with students, essentially as lenses through which to investigate the nature of and responses to historical change. In so doing, they follow in the History Workshop tradition of concern with the experiential. Material culture is one of the 'vantage points' used in Public History from which to explore a personalised past.

As totems of conviction in, or fear of, the future, contemporary collectables and the numerous magazines which document them are a rich source of contemporary history and cultural information. The Museum, as historically the officially sanctioned state collector of artefacts, has made a response to this activity in the form of the 'People's Show' in which the collections of the individual are collectively displayed in museum space.[22] An MA class visit to one such exhibition, along with some contextual reading, led to much useful and interesting discussion and debate.[23] The student previously mentioned used the personal insight gained through this to research and write up aspects of her family history. Popular collecting can be read as a material cultural form of 'mass observation', and works in tandem with oral history in that each collection is a narrative of the collector themself.[24] This is why historians of the late twentieth century must look to additional sources other than printed documentary evidence. As Asa Briggs has noted: 'Memories and myths are strong in Sunday colour supplements, figuring not only in articles but in the advertisements that serve as their main rationale. Taken together they express the unique balance in English history between continuity and change'.[25] Whilst some students were uncomfortable with the idea of collecting as a process or activity per se, others found in it a deeper meaning to the objects which they themselves collected. In the process, it also developed an interesting debate on the nature of work and leisure activity, and the way in which they were no longer necessarily mutually separate spheres. Hobbies in many instances come to be a means of earning income as 'the job' as we have always understood it rapidly disappears.[26] Perhaps this is one area in which public history is a step forward from the original History Workshop. The boundaries that once delineated the structures of class, gender, work, leisure etc. in conventional popular cultural history are no longer as obvious as once they were, and needed to be re-addressed and interpreted. In essence, Raph's acceptance and validation of my Ruskin project all those years ago has acted as a constant reminder of how much meaning and insight can be gained from the superficially inconsequential. Raph showed me how to deconstruct the visual, aural and oral, and that virtually everything had at least one metanarrative. I am now able to encourage my own students to do likewise.

All of this may be taken as symbolic of how the popular

informs and even revises the rarefied. A table of binary opposites gives some examples:

Figure 1: Table of binary opposites

Rarefied domain	Popular domain
archaeology	metal detecting
elite biography	family history
classical ('serious') music	popular music
academic journals	popular magazines
classical literature	pulp fiction
antique appreciation	popular collecting

What has happened during the 1990s is that much of what appears under the first heading has sought to democratise itself by addressing itself to wider audiences which appear under the second. Archaeology, for example, despite a tradition of inclusiveness in terms of participation in digs etc., never had a truly populist profile until the advent of Channel Four's *Time Team* series in the mid-1990s.[27] Attempts to embrace a wider audience for classical music have ranged from the pairing of classical music excerpts with disco rhythms in the early 1980s, to the promotion of opera singers as pop stars, and their utilisation of operatic excerpts for sporting and other mass audience events, whilst the *Antiques Roadshow*, over two decades, has brought previously 'sacred' knowledge to a popular audience. Effectively then, these serve as public history sources which show how knowledge is gained outside of the academy, and are drawn on in the pursuit of opening wider avenues of conceptual historical understanding.

In its first year, one student found the visual culture module especially helpful. She had been left a group of photographs by her father, just before his death, which seemed to be of key moments in his life. However, he did not leave any written information as to their importance to him. The module helped the student to analyse and interpret them to some satisfaction. This resulted in an excellent dissertation on the subject and process.[28]

The visual is one focus of the MA, the aural is another.[29] The popular music session on the MA looks at a number of issues: What do we mean by 'popular' music?[30] How and why has the popular music of the past become fashionable again?[31] and what cultural and historical meaning is there in the changes in technology?[32] What we discover in exploring such questions are the changes (or resistance to them) in attitudes and perceptions. These offer a way in which we can come to understand our life experience as history, and through which we can understand the process of change.

REGGAE, SOUL, ROCK 'N' ROLL, JAZZ, FUNK, PUNK

Pop music is as public as can be got in terms of a subject. In recent years changes in its production and consumption offer a fertile site for the study of changes in popular perception. Musically, 'popular' is perceived as anything from Cole Porter to The Spice Girls, though it can also mean minority musics which have for whatever reason now become more commercial through various media usage, be they of the past or the present. This thus suggests that sound is as semantic as the spoken word, and worthy of being 'read' as a 'text'. Those who desired 'serious' (classical) music to remain a bastion of cultural snobbery had their prejudices reinforced and accepted as received wisdom in previous decades, because classical music was perceived as unchanging, whilst 'pop' (as in youth) music was perceived as faddish and disposable.[33] By now however, 1950s blues music has been used for advertising, for example, Miller beer (Howling Wolf's *Smokestack Lightnin'*) or Levi jeans (Muddy Waters' *Manish Boy*), as has contemporary pop and rock, whilst classical music is used as incidental and background sound in any number of instances. Advertisers seek to convey, and identify with the product advertised, notions of consistency, constancy and simple pleasures, or evoke mood through classical music's use. Musically then, advertising cuts and pastes the past, purging it of context, using it to underline the present, irrespective of its genre. Half a century after the birth of rock'n'roll, pop is an art form as institutional as classical, jazz or any other music. As an exercise in the study of cultural appropriation, it links contemporary public history with the mission of History Workshop to find connections and make distinction in otherwise hegomonic perceptions.

The institutional overexposure of well known pop songs and the tendency of contemporary popular music to lend itself too easily to such (ab)use led to disenchantment amongst many people. On the one hand a search for new musical expression led to the dance/rave/junglist cultures of the 1990s, and on the other, and to some extent in conjunction with the former, it led to a reassessment of older musics, such as 1960s soul and 1970s funk. This older music could then be repositioned as novel again. From around 1987, the disc jockey began to become more than a player of records in club culture, and started to become a producer and mixer of records, often comprised of samples from other records.[34] By the early 1990s, the use of digital sampling machines had become a sub-genre of its own in popular music. James Brown, the 'godfather of soul', is often stated to be 'the most sampled man in show business' (after his original reputation as the hardest working man in show business). With advances in technology, DJs became a kind of surrogate musician by proxy, via their skills at a mixing desk. Their knowledge and use of old records, and the preference of many rap and hip-hop performers for samples of old records, represented the old as new to a new generation of young club goers. In this way, curiosity was aroused in the young about the music of the past, causing many to search out original records of which they had heard samples. This served to stimulate the reissues market in CDs, which also appealed to older music consumers who remembered the music first time round, and this helped in its turn to revamp older music scenes such as Northern Soul.[35] The formal and perfunctory sleeve notes on the back of vinyl LPs at their original time of issue have long been superseded by copious historical essays in the form of the accompanying booklet in their CD reissue format. In addition, popular music magazines such as *Mojo*, which have an older readership (typically 25-50), address the historical as much as the contemporary. This is (high) street level public history, which exists independently of the body of academic sociological literature on popular music which has also mushroomed over the last two decades. The musical past is here actively sought out and thus 'learned', rather than being selectively imposed and 'assumed'. In the process we all to some extent become historians, a concept that Raph would certainly have appreciated.[36]

The popular reception of technological change in recent years is also pertinent. The model used to explore this has been the replacement of analogue by digital recording techniques, and vinyl records by the compact disc.[37] Over the last fifteen years, there has emerged a culture of militant particularism as a result of this technological change. The death of vinyl was almost a given as digital technology brought the Compact Disc to prominence in the mid-1980s. However, there has been a very strong resurgence of adherence to vinyl in recent years by young music lovers. Therefore, can anything inherent in the vinyl format be found which symbolises a deeper significance to attachment to it? What we find is a poetic and sensory approach to this historical divergence. A short film on the subject, as part of the BBC's Windrush season, illustrates rather nicely how this works.[38] Joyce James came to Britain from Trinidad in 1954. She has a large collection of vinyl LPs and 78rpm records. Her husband (now dead) was a great Earl Bostic fan (an American rhythm and blues and jazz saxophonist) and bought lots of his records. When she listens to the songs, it makes her homesick (for Trinidad). Her husband came home one day having bought six Earl Bostic records, costing a total of 24/-. She argued with him about it: '24 shillings was a lot of money then' ... 'we used to enjoy our records though'. She polishes her 78 rpm records, laying them on top of each other, interleaved with kitchen roll. Some of these have long been broken: 'Although I know I can never play them ... just so long as it's there, I go through the song in my head'. In this case, the broken record, a useless functional object, rubbish in fact, is a powerful signifier, a memory cue for the context in which it was obtained and the history which it connotes for her. To own it on CD would not do because as an *object* it would not be original to the period in time from which the music comes.

There is an even stronger sensory ritual associated with ownership of vinyl, felt to be lacking in CD, which two other contributors to the Windrush film acknowledge. One, DJ Pogo, describes: 'The aroma of it. It's just a smell that is very, very distinctive; nothing else smells like it. Stale vinyl, stale paper, even if it's new it will have a smell about it'. Camille, another contributor states that:

> When you buy a record, there's a whole kind of ritual of holding it and actually breaking the plastic seal, and actually getting the vinyl out. And obviously, because obviously it's brand new, no-one else has touched this record, it's kind of new, crisp, untouched, only by yourself, so it's quite mad really.

Similarly, John Walters, a Radio One programme producer, sits amongst his collection of 12,500 vinyl records decrying the compact disc, whilst equating the vinyl with life experience:

> It's like taking a Brillo pad to a Rembrandt. No, this is the way it should be: mono, vinyl. Smells like vinyl, tastes of vinyl. People will say 'it's got a few scratches and clicks on that though'. Then life's got a few scratches and clicks.[39]

Also in the Windrush film we find a specialist reggae record shop (Dub Vendor) owner, Don Facey, making the point that: 'record shops were a water hole for new arrivals in Britain'. It was somewhere where they could find news about home and form friendships through music, and get to know the community. Indeed, secondary market record shops, genre or theme specific music clubs, and changes in the attitude of music consumers as vinyl gave way to compact disc, all become points of departure in attitude and therefore historical and cultural movement.[40]

Indeed one student wrote his dissertation on collecting records in which he explored the ways in which vinyl and CD coexisted how different musical genres (e.g. classical and heavy metal) made use of them and how they were marketed.[41] Another student, who was for a time a successful musician in the 1960s, and for whom the new interest in old music was a particular puzzle, wrote an essay on his musical experiences, using music as a way to structure his experience historically.

The foregoing has been related to demonstrate the way in which aspects of Ruskin history are addressing the recent as much as the more distant past, and the continuity between the conceptual ideas of the original History Workshop and some current interpretations of what history *can be*. Having done so, it is I feel, appropriate to end in much the same way that I started, with a Ruskin remembrance. I do so as a means of relating the examples given back to the educational crucible which first afforded me the opportunity to develop them. In so doing, I hope that something of the process by which Ruskin students develop comes through.

THE LONG GOODBYE 1: RUSKIN MEMORIES

My Ruskin generation arrived in Oxford a motley crew of industrial refugees. Our number was formed from ex's: men were ex miners, printers and engineers, whilst amongst the women were ex factory, textile and clothing industry workers. This was 1986, the period of 'high Thatcherism', and we typified the backgrounds that Hilda Kean in her chapter notes as characteristic of Ruskin students. She also notes the record of Ruskin student dissenting activity. The preceding generation had been involved locally with the miners' strike; my generation were to be involved in the Wapping dispute, anti-apartheid movement and demonstrations against the health cuts. We had a large collective chip on our shoulders about Oxford and what it stood for. We made friends with the local trades union council, initially adopting a town rather than gown stance. Hilda Kean in her chapter notes that, apart from Ruskin, none of the Oxford colleges displays its name. This appeared to us as a deliberate conspiratorial anonymity, in order to deter 'us Judes' from approaching. The chip, however, was soon knocked off, as many joined the Oxford Union and attended lectures at other colleges. On the other hand there was a different story when we were parading into the Bodleian library to swear the oath not to burn the place down ('I promise not to kindle any flame within the confines' or some such). We were all sitting on a bench awaiting our turn to take the oath. One student had inadvertently left his student card behind and could not be 'sworn in'. He stormed out muttering that he was not bothered, as the whole place was only six hundred years of ritual designed to oppress the working class. As he did so, we struck up a 'choral hum' of the 'Red Flag' in his honour. On only our third day, a scratch Ruskin football team full of beer-bellied men was fielded against a sprightly university side of eighteen-year-olds. I was roped in as referee, and a poor one – I was unaware of the rules of play, not being a sporting type. What was most noticeable about our side was their aggression against their opponent's shins, and whereas the opposition had half-time oranges, Ruskin had a half-time fag break, amongst much wheezing and searching for breath! Ultimately, we all adjusted.

Hilda Kean notes in her chapter the frequency with which former students defined the Ruskin experience as a transformation. Rather like football managers who are 'over the moon' at good results, or rock groups who split up over 'musical differences', this has become something of a cliché, simply because it best sums up the experience. There is, however, another way in which Ruskin acts as a site. It is a site of the making and breaking of personal relationships. What is opportunity for those leaving for Ruskin is often only sacrifice for those they leave behind. On a vertical time line, the student's relationship with the past from the vantage point of the present is a positive engagement, the reason for being at Ruskin, and is strengthened accordingly. On a horizontal timeline between those who leave and those who are left behind, it represents disengagement. It is a timeline of regretted absence and distance. It is this that can cause such organic linkages to break, and which is sometimes the real cost of a Ruskin education. One ex-Ruskin student of the 1920s recalled:

> For women folk coming to Ruskin, it was really terrible. When they went back to their husbands they'd had two years at Oxford, two years education, all the atmosphere of Oxford. Then they'd go back to a husband who hadn't moved at all, and so really, it broke up the family. There was quite a lot of break up of marriages as a result of it, there's no question about that.[42]

Even in the 1980s, Ruskin, staff noted, still had a reputation for its detrimental effects on personal relationships.

THE LONG GOODBYE 2: AFTER RUSKIN

In 1988 I proceeded from Ruskin to Sussex University, to study history and cultural and community studies (CCS). Under the tutelage of another History Workshop stalwart and ex-Ruskin student, Alun Howkins, then senior lecturer in history and for a time Dean of CCS, I found the Ruskin ethos coming through, just as strongly. At Sussex, a small colony of Ruskin graduates from the class of '88 could be found in different disciplines. What we all agreed on was the confidence Ruskin had given us, which became apparent when we found ourselves in university seminar groups with younger undergraduates. We would often be the first to proffer our analysis or opinion on a question, often we would be the only ones to do so. We felt perhaps that we were inhibiting younger students from speaking, so we tried to hold back. We then found they did not speak much anyway, so we than felt that they were perhaps hiding behind us. We did not realise that it was taking a lot longer for them to find the confidence that we had by now come to take for granted. Two years of block meetings in Bowen at the Headington site, and Kitson at the town centre site, in which long nights were spent in the kitchens over numerous cups of coffee and tea, putting the world to rights, had helped me hone my argumentative and reasoning powers without even realising it.

All those optional models undertaken such as Bill Hughes public speaking and Brian Spittles's film analysis had added to the brew. The droll and often witty criticism of Victor Treadwell and Harold Pollins of what I had struggled with for days, even weeks sometimes, to put into writing, I found ultimately to be beneficial in that it caused me to be more self critical in my academic thinking. The copious photocopies from books and journals, patiently located by those bastions of student friendly librarianship, David and Val Horsfield, were all to prove their use. Looming over it all, was the memory of Raph, because it had been he who had (unknowingly) made such a positive impression on me when I first came to Ruskin. His passing came at a time when other historians I had known and admired also sadly left us.[43] This all seemed at the time as though it were the passing of an era. I felt that the world could not afford to lose people such as these, because they stood for what humanises it and values the most positive elements of our nature. I still feel that. It is what History Workshop and Ruskin history has always sought to do. However, I was pleased to hear the same comments, opinions and attitudes from current students about their Ruskin experience, that I felt about my own.

Ruskin was always special to itself, even when residential adult education colleges were a little thicker on the ground than they now are. A higher education institution, it is in other respects viewed as a further education institution for the benefit of complying with pre set categories, none of which Ruskin quite fits into. Perhaps this is just something peculiarly 'Oxford'. Ruskin people turn up everywhere. During my doctoral research in museum studies at Leicester University, a couple turned up on the Museum Studies M.A. course I was teaching there, and somehow knew I was of their number. I well remember Raph musing over whom he knew at various colleges and universities to whom he could recommend some Ruskin graduate, he seemed to know everyone in one way or another. I still like to think of Ruskin graduates infiltrating and subverting the structures they enter into in some small way at least, imbuing it with a little of the Ruskin spirit.

Raph was a totem for many Ruskin students. He was often their first encounter with academia and gave them the confidence to pursue and importantly, to enjoy reading and writing in ways they would not have thought themselves capable of. The general environment at Ruskin was and continues to be a nurturing and empowering one. Ruskin history continues to emphasise and value the common ownership of history in which we are all a part. In this sense at least, Raph's presence still resides at Ruskin.

NOTES

1. Coincidentally, now being resurrected and expanded for publication as *The Trade Union Badge - Material Culture In Action* (in preparation).
2. R. Samuel (ed), *History Workshop: A Collectanea 1967-1997*, History Workshop, London, 1997.

3. S. Rowbotham, 'Remembering 1967 Sheila Rowbotham (interviewed 19 October 1991)', in Samuel 1997, *op.cit.*, p3.

4. Editorial Collective, 'Editorials', *History Workshop Journal*, No.1, spring 1976, p2.

5. *Ibid.*

6. *Ibid.*, p3.

7. A. Light, S. Alexander, G. Steadman Jones, R. Samuel (eds), *Island Stories: Unravelling Britain*, Verso, London 1998, p222.

8. *Ibid.*, pp222-3.

9. B. Goldstone, 'Out takes', *Independent Saturday Magazine*, 20 December 1997, p46; B.Goldstone & A. Goldstone, *The Los Angeles Watts Tower*, Thames & Hudson, London 1997. See also M. Davies, *City of Quartz: Excavating the Future in Los Angeles*, Verso, London 1990 (especially pp373-441) in which the popular mythology and reality of Los Angeles are analysed.

10. R. Cardinal, 'Collecting and Collage-Making: The Case of Kurt Schwitters' in J. Elsner and R. Cardinal (eds), *The Cultures of Collecting*, Reaktion, London 1994, pp68-96, see p74 for illustration.

11. *Ibid.*, p72.

12. R. Wells, 'What a Load of Rubbish!', *Evergreen*, Autumn 1995, pp118-121, p119

13. *Ibid.*, p118.

14. See for instance R. Samuel, *Theatres of Memory Vol.1: Past and Present in Contemporary Culture*, Verso, London 1995.

15. A. Roberts, 'Historians agog over can labels', *The Times*, 27 May 1993.

16. That the objects were often seen as more than just decorative is implied in the formation of collectors clubs, such as the 'League of Goss Collectors' (crested china) which existed from 1900 until the Goss company's demise in 1932.

17. Samuel 1995, *op.cit.*.

18. National Council For Metal Detecting, *A Shared Heritage*, Newbury, Berkshire 1992, p3.

19. R. Belk, *Collecting in a Consumer Society*, Routledge, London 1995; S.M. Pearce, *On Collecting*, Routledge, London 1995; S.M. Pearce, *Collecting in Contemporary Practice*, Sage, London 1998; P. Martin, *Popular Collecting and the Everyday Self: The Reinvention of Museums?*, Leicester University Press, London 1999.

20. R. Belk, 'Possessions and the Extended Self', *Journal of Consumer Research*, Vol.15, 1988, pp139-168; S. Lancaster & M. Foddy, 'Self Extensions: A Conceptualization', *Journal for the Theory of Social Behaviour*,18:1, 1988, pp77-94.

21. P. Martin, 'Tomorrow's History Today: Postmodern Collecting', *History Today*, Vol.46 (2), February 1996, pp5-8; P. Martin, *Popular Collecting*, *op.cit.*.

22. J. Digger, *The People's Show at Walsall*, unpublished M.A. thesis, Dept. Museum Studies, University of Leicester, 1995; R. Fardell, *From Australiana to World War Memorabilia: The People's Show Festival at Harborough Museum*, unpublished M.A. thesis, Dept. Museum Studies, Leicester University, 1995; R. Fardell, 'The People's Show Festival 1994 At Harborough Museum', *Museological Review*, Vol.1, No.2, 1995, pp72-76; J.R. Lovatt, 'A People's Show *Means* A People's Show', *Museological Review*, Vol.1, No.2, 1995, pp66-71; J.R. Lovatt, 'The People's Show Festival 1994', in S.M. Pearce (ed), *Experiencing Material Culture in the Western World*, Leicester University Press, London 1997, pp196-254.

23. The Museum of Collectors, The Barge House, Oxo Tower Wharf, South Bank, London 13.11.98–6.3.99. See also, J. Griffiths, 'You Are What You Keep', *Guardian (G2)*, 10 November 1998, pp8-9; S. Smith, 'Comparing Notes', *Collect It!*, January 1999, pp67-69.

24. J. Baudrillard, 'The Systems Of Collecting' in Elsner and Cardinal, *op.cit.*, Reaktion Books, London 1994, pp7-24.

25. A. Briggs, 'The 1990s – The Final Chapter' in A. Briggs & D. Snowman (eds), *Fins de Siecle: How Centuries End, 1400-2000*, Yale University Press, London 1996, p225 See also Asa Briggs, *Victorian Things*, Penguin, London (2nd edition), 1990 as an example of how the material culture of the everyday has been used to unfold academic history. Briggs was president of the Ephemera Society.

26. See for instance R.A. Stebbins, 'Serious Leisure: A Conceptual Statement', *Pacific Sociological Review*, No.25, April 1982, pp251-272; E.A.Christ, 'The Retired Stamp Collector: economic and other functions of a systematized leisure activity' in A.R. Rose and W.A. Peterson (eds), *Older People and Their Social World: The Subculture of Ageing*, F.A. Davies Publishers, Philadelphia 1965, pp93-112.

27. For instance an article of the early 1980s attacking metal detecting also asserts: 'Archaeology is now, and has always been, a largely middle class pursuit'. It also makes the case for popular archaeology in the wake of interest in the raising of the Mary Rose. T. Gregory, 'The Impact of Metal Detecting on Archaeology and the Public', *Archaeological Review From Cambridge*, Vol.2, Part 1, spring 1983, pp5-8.

28. S. Morgan, *My Father's Photographs: The Mnemonic Artefact and Family Memory*, M.A. dissertation, Ruskin College, Oxford 1998, pp1-6. Morgan sees the photographs as an already authored informal history to which she is adding and continuing through her own analysis. She holds them to have

meaning beyond personal family history in that they are vernacular cultural productions enabling us to site connections between broad change and the experience of it. This is perhaps the very essence of Raph's philosophy and Ruskin history.

29. There is already a successful contextual module on blues music being run by Mavis Bayton on the CHE.

30. A question posited in one of the exhibition rooms at Sheffield's National Centre For Popular Music, which asks the visitor to consider the nature of 'throw away' pop and 'durable' rock.

31. For example, the revival in popularity of older popular musics includes: jive and jump blues of the late 1940s and early 1950s, see A. Gentleman, 'Young professionals switch on to jive as lindy hop hits Britain', *Guardian* 17.10.98, p3; and 1960s Northern Soul, see R. Johnson, 'Soul Survivors', *Guardian Weekend* 6.2.99, pp42-45.

32. The most obvious change is in the overall sound and design by production techniques. Examples of innovative record producers such as Phil Spector are internationally known. Others include British producer Joe Meek in pop music of the early 1960s; see J. Repsch, *The Legendary Joe Meek, The Telstar Man*, Woodford House, London 1989. Reggae for instance boasts such legends as Clement 'Coxone' Dodd, Duke Reid, Prince Buster, Lee Perry and King Tubby. See S. Barrow and P. Dalton, *Reggae: The Rough Guide*, Rough Guides, London 1997.

33. Even the study of the history and changes in jazz (outside of individual biographies of musicians), which most closely resembles classical music in terms of 'appreciation' and artistic validation, is a contemporary trend. See for instance: R. Kennedy, *Jelly Roll, Bix and Hoagy: Gennett Studios and the Birth of Recorded Jazz*, Indiana University Press, Bloomington and Indianapolis, 1994; David Stowe, *Swing Changes: Big Band Jazz In New Deal America*, Harvard University Press, Cambridge, Massachusetts and London 1994.

34. U. Poschardt, Shaun Whiteside (translator), *D.J. Culture*, Quartet, London 1998, p216.

35. See for instance: P. McKenna, *Nightshift*, STP Publishing, Argyll 1996; R. Winstanley and D. Nowell, *Soul Survivors: The Wigan Casino Story*, Robson Books, London 1996.

36. See for instance R. Samuel 1995, *op.cit.*, and *Island Stories*, 1998, *op.cit.*.

37. For a detailed history of recorded music see A. Millard, *America On Record: A History of Recorded Sound*, Cambridge University Press, Cambridge 1995.

38. *A Little Piece of Home* (Windrush season), BBC2 28.8.98. A series of short films looking at the Afro-Caribbean experience in Britain since 1948.

39. *The Antiques Show*, BBC2, 11 May 1999. For further comment on the vinyl vs CD debate see T. Cox, 'Full Circle', *Guardian* 20.10.98, pp4-5. Similarly, Dennis Chiles, a former Ruskin student and principal of Plater College, Oxford, recalled an instance in which he encountered Raph with his arms full of old books, the virtues of which he began to extol. Raph apparently implored him to hug them and smell them, to love them simply because they were old books and should therefore be cherished (conversation, Ruskin College, May 1999). On a different subject, one Ruskin student was partly moved to write his dissertation project from the recollection of the taste of a stick of chewing gum given to him by an American G.I in Belfast when a child in the early 1950s.

40. P. Martin, work in progress.

41. J. Foot, *Record Collecting And Recycling In The Music Industry*, M.A., Ruskin College, Oxford 1998.

42. The same ex-student recalled the case of a fellow female student who, after her time at Ruskin in which she had naturally progressed, returned to work on the factory floor and the routine of her former job. The effect of which, after her time in Oxford, led her to commit suicide. The early ethos of Ruskin was for students on completion of their courses to return to the workplace to disseminate their learning amongst their workplace peers. Naturally, this would not be what many wanted. *Ruskin At 100*, BBC Radio 4, broadcast 11 February 1999.

43. Eddie Frow at the Working Class Movement Library (WCML) in Salford, who with his wife Ruth, had been a prime mover in compiling a hugely culturally valuable collection of working-class literature from the eighteenth to twentieth centuries; John Gorman, a key contributor to working-class visual history. His books included *Banner Bright*, Scorpion, London, 1972 and 1986; *To Build Jerusalem*, Scorpion, London, 1980; *Images Of Labour*, Scorpion, London 1985. Also a lesser known individual, John Hammond. Hammond had been the founder of the Trade Union Badge Collectors' Society, and had compiled a comprehensive catalogue of all known British trade union badges. He and the society worked in conjunction with the WCML and the National Museum of Labour History in Manchester over the years, and he would have been exactly the sort of person Raph would have valued.

The place of Ruskin in its own history

HILDA KEAN

When Harold Pollins wrote his history of Ruskin College in 1984 he cited nearly ninety publications all covering in their subject matter aspects of the history of Ruskin College.[1] Within this 'genre', autobiographies of former students feature prominently. Certainly much has been written, particularly by former students, defining Ruskin College as a site of personal transformation. Recent written testimonies in the brochure for the centenary gala and taped interviews made on the day by Bill Whitehead continue to employ this motif to describe time spent at Ruskin. For Philip Elliot, a student between 1955 and 1957, 'Ruskin was a turning point in my life. Without that experience and its continuing friendships, the turbulent journey of 45 years since would have been even more difficult to navigate'.[2] Many of the former students interviewed by Bill Whitehead attended Ruskin in the 1990s. Unprompted many also used the language of transformation, so common in their predecessor's descriptions, to describe their experience: 'Ruskin changed my life for the better'; 'I was lucky to be here, it changed my life a lot'.[3]

THE PHYSICAL SITING OF RUSKIN COLLEGE

In this chapter I want to explore Ruskin College as a site of such narratives, as a physical presence which has apparently impacted so significantly on the lives of those who have lived and studied there. In doing this I want to look at the ways in which the physicality of the place itself has been developed and contested by those studying and employed within its walls. Since 1912 Ruskin College has occupied its current building in central Oxford at the corner of Worcester Place and Walton Street. Its physical location and the architectural form of the building might tell us much about the broader political and academic location of the College. As Raphael Samuel suggested, 'The idea of getting buildings to tell a story, and of using them as mnemonic devices, to teach history, mythologize rulers and commemorate great events, is as old as the Pharaohs of Egypt'.[4] The institution was founded in 1899 by three Americans, Walter Vrooman, Amne Vrooman (née Grafflin) and Charles Beard. The site of the inaugural public meeting is itself telling. The event was not held in the university's Sheldonian theatre but the premier building of the town, Oxford Town Hall. This bridging of place between two different sorts of Oxford is also embodied in the location of the main college building. On one side set back from the street is Worcester College with its splendid Georgian edifice looking down towards the first public museum in Britain, the Ashmolean, and the Martyrs' memorial. On the other side is Jericho, traditionally an area of skilled working-class people. It was in this area that Thomas Hardy set his novel *Jude the Obscure*, in which the stonemason Jude travelled to the fictionalised Oxford with the thwarted hope of achieving a formal classical education. With its red brick workers' cottages, Worcester Place itself also presented a coming together of different Oxfords as can be explored through the census returns detailing the occupations of the residents. In the late nineteenth century it housed many whose jobs reflected the market town of Oxford: ironmonger's apprentice, hide skin auctioneer, butcher, veterinary surgeon's assistant and house decorator. But many others living in the street depended on the presence of the University for their livelihoods such as a bookbinder, photographer's assistant, library assistant, compositor, and college servant.[5]

The site of Ruskin College itself was acquired from the wealthy St John's College, the landlord of the extravagant housing developments in North Oxford, particularly the prestigious Park Town estate. In style the building looked to the university. As the

College governing body saw it, 'The new buildings present a handsome frontage to Walton Street. They are Georgian in design, and are a worthy addition to the many beautiful buildings in Oxford'.[6]

Ironically, even if the College had been built to the original plans it is unlikely that its edifice would have received the approval of the College's namesake John Ruskin, who had clear views of the purpose of architecture. Any building, according to John Ruskin, needed to do three things: act well and do the things it was intended to do in the best way; speak well, and say the things it was intended to say in the best words; look well and please us by its presence, whatever it has to do or say.[7]

While the new building clearly pleased the governors, whether it conveyed its intention 'in the best way' is less certain. For John Ruskin the visual informed the verbal and there was a direct correlation between the condition of art and the health of a nation.[8] Were the mixed messages conveyed by the architecture and iconography reflecting the contemporary state of the College or rather what the governors hoped it might be? The governors admired the mock Georgian facade, overlooking a subtle but important difference with classic Georgian buildings. Unlike the facade of adjacent Worcester College the top half of Ruskin was – and still is – built of red brick, the same material used in the workers' cottages in Worcester Place. This is not an imposing building set back from the day to day bustle of Oxford streets. Above the main entrance is a stone crest but, in marked contrast to the practice of Oxford colleges, the name of the College is included. The very fact that the name was included set the College apart from those it emulated. There is traditionally no reference to the name of the College on Oxford University buildings. (Presumably if you do not know instinctively, through genetics and breeding, what the building is then you have no right to be there.) Instead Ruskin presents itself in the style of nineteenth-century mechanics' institutes ; the institutional character now reinforced by both the steps up to the entrance and the raised ground level windows. In its physical facade the building reflected two distinct traditions: the long established elite Oxford college and the mechanics' institutes aimed ostensibly at working-class people.

The facade of Ruskin College, Walton Street.
Photo, Hilda Kean.

The intention was to present a building which seemed to have been part of the fabric of Oxford for considerably longer than a mere thirteen years. Certainly the early years of the College were characterised by financial insecurity and concerns about the long-term viability of the venture. The building was set against such uncertainty. With the four stone plaques under the College windows there was an attempt to create a permanence and sense of longevity. The engraved names are of Amne Grafflin, former wife of another founder, Walter Vrooman, and chief benefactor of the early years;[9] Miss Giles, a member of staff since the founding of the College; Charles Bowerman, the TUC president in 1901, Labour MP, early supporter and Ruskin executive committee member and Sydney Buxton, the Liberal MP and father of the former vice- principal. The engraving of the names in stone served to commemorate both the links with the past founders, trade union links, and the continuing present particularly through the staff who had kept the place going in difficult times.[10] With this new building the College was starting to create for itself a specific historical identity reflecting a state of permanence.

EDUCATIONAL AND HISTORICAL ORIGINS

The contradictory meanings in the new building epitomised the educational problematic underpinning the College itself. The college had distinguished itself from the university by the adoption of its name in homage to John Ruskin who had famously argued that in order for education to be given usefully, 'it should be clearly understood to be no means of getting on in the world, but a means of staying pleasantly in your place there'.[11] Specifically John Ruskin rejected accomplishments in Latin or dainty manners as a sign of education: 'A man is ... only educated if he is happy, busy, beneficent, and effective in the world. Millions of peasants are, therefore, at this moment better educated than most of those who call themselves gentlemen'.[12]

Speaking at the founding meeting of the College in February 1899 Walter Vrooman had declared in similar vein that there 'was not only one, there were many true educations, as many as there were different functions in society'. The education which would be offered by the College would be deliberately different to that of the university. Students would come to Ruskin, 'not as mendicant pilgrims went to Jerusalem, to worship at her ancient shrines and marvel at her sacred relics, but as Paul went to Rome, to conquer in a battle of ideas'.[13] But despite the early statements, since those heady days of 1899 the College had undergone much turmoil and dissent precisely over the type of education to be taught in the College. The new building was planned for and erected after the defeat of the Ruskin strike of 1909 which had drawn sharp divisions on the nature of education the College was offering.[14] There were pithy slogans on both sides of the dispute. 'Do you suffer from class consciousness? Come to Oxford and be cured', allegedly cried the Syndicalist strikers.[15] In different vein Henry Sanderson Furniss, a contemporary tutor and subsequent principal, recalled his time at the College, 'I had never read a line of Marx. I knew very little of the Socialist writers and those I had read had made no impression on my mind. I had hardly ever spoken to a working man except gardeners, coachmen, and game-keepers.'[16]

After the dismissal of Dennis Hird (and the establishment of the Central Labour College in London which he then ran, as a Marxist alternative to Ruskin), there was a consolidation of a closer working relationship with the university. From 1910 students began to sit the Oxford University Diploma in Economics and Political Science, attend university lectures, use the Bodleian library and speak at Oxford Union debates.[17]

Within the students' studies – as well as in the building – there was a keen awareness of the importance of history established from the very earliest years. Under the memorandum of association drawn up to register the College under the Companies Act it had been declared that the College should provide instruction in history, modern languages and science, the duties of a citizen and practical industrial work. (As an implicit critique of the university curriculum and in the spirit of John Ruskin, at no time would there be the teaching of dead languages (Latin, Greek or Hebrew), metaphysics, party politics or theology.[18]) The inclusion of history was no accident. Charles Beard, who was to become a leading historian, 'foremost among the American historians of his or any other generation in the search for a usable past',[19] had met Walter Vrooman while studying European and English History in England.[20] Two specific courses in history were offered in the first prospectus of the College in 1899: English and Constitutional History and Industrial History. Indeed the inaugural lecture at the College in 1899 was delivered by Charles Beard on English constitutional history.[21]

This interest in history was reflected in a concern for an historical identity which implicitly conveyed a sense of continuity within the building's interior. The fabric and iconography of the building itself became a protagonist in structuring the discourse of educational and political debates. Until recently, looking at the physical appearance of the main building alone, new students and visitors alike would no doubt have formed the impression of a staid and uninterrupted tradition. This sense of tradition was conveyed primarily through the naming of rooms and the installation of plaques in commemoration of bygone heroes. Public rooms were named after men with former links with the College including Herbert Elvin, the general secretary of the Clerks' Union, member of the governing council, and father of a former college principal and Charles Buxton in whose memory the new lecture hall built in 1913 was named. A splendid wrought black metal plate was erected over the hall's side entrance in iconography more commonly reserved for the war dead. Indeed in the early 1990s the only postcard of the College available for purchase was of an unrefurbished Buxton hall: formal rows of empty chairs recalling in a nostalgic mood a faded minor public school.

DISSENTING POLITICS: CONTESTING IDENTITIES

Of the past disruption and oppositional activities in the College there was no permanent recognition. The action of students in the 1990s in inviting outside speakers unfashionable in the new labour world, including Tony Benn, Arthur Scargill and Liz Davies, one of the few left-wing members of the NEC of the Labour Party, is not a new phenomenon. In the 1920s Ruskin provided a hall for speakers, such as Marie Stopes and Bertrand Russell, barred from speaking within the university because of their unfashionable views.[22] Students certainly have a record of dissenting activity: anti-fascist activity in the 1930s when they formed themselves into red-shirts to oppose fascists organising in the university;[23] solidarity with the miners in the strikes of the last three decades; recent support for asylum seekers and refugees and perhaps most significantly the hosting of the first women's liberation movement conference in Britain in February 1970. Some written testimonies which have appeared in recent years from participants at the Women's Liberation Movement conference have looked at the conflict emanating from the contradiction between the political substance of the conference and the ideas inherent within its physical location. In her account of the event, Sally Alexander, then a history student at Ruskin, presented a story not so much of an important event but one which was born out of struggle with an antagonistic environment of hostile college authorities – and students. The idea for the conference had arisen from a History Workshop conference during which a number of women had sought to arrange a meeting with others engaged in women's history. Despite the derision with which this idea was met by some participants, the conference did indeed take place, not in London where the embryonic movement was making strides, but in Ruskin College. This was apparently welcomed less than enthusiastically by the College authorities and with hostility by many male students.[24]

While the College was pleased to host a conference in 1990 celebrating the impact of women's liberation twenty years on, there was no attempt to commemorate the initial event within the permanent fittings of the building.[25] Certainly, although the College has taught women students since its founding – one of its earliest correspondence students being the suffrage feminist leader Annie Kenney – their presence and that of female members of staff has not been historicised in the same way as that of male dignitaries. No room has been named after Grace Coleman, the first woman tutor, in economics, and subsequent Labour MP for Tynemouth in 1945, nor after the women members of the governing council, Margaret Bondfield, the first woman to serve in a Labour cabinet, nor Mary MacArthur, the leader of the National Federation of Women Workers, which sponsored two of the first women residential students at the College in the 1920s.[26] An effect of this failure to 'historicise' the continuing presence of women within the College has been to describe events covering women as new, 'firsts for the College'. While the celebration of women's achievements is, of course, welcome, it also suggests erroneously that women have not been an integral part of the institution. Our role is then seen as apart from the tradition of the College and outside the ongoing work of Ruskin and thus easier to marginalise in the present. When Women's Studies was first introduced as a subject for the Certificate of Higher Education in 1993 some saw this as a new venture in that numbers of women would attend the College. That women had been attending the College as residential students for over seventy years seemed to have been forgotten.[27] The effect of absence within the built environment was to highlight some moments in the historical past while consigning others to oblivion.[28]

This institutional amnesia has been disputed in recent years by students themselves insisting on challenging the absence of women in the iconography of the building. The rooms in which students were taught themselves became an issue. As part of the celebrations on International Women's Day in 1995 rooms were (temporarily) redesignated in honour of Women against Pit Closures, Southall Black Sisters, and Lesbian Avengers. Subsequently montages of women students have been constructed by the students themselves; one adorned the entrance hall and was then sold as an official greetings card. As part of the current centenary celebrations women students have organised a decorative panel to ensure that there is a permanent reminder of their role within the building.

Changes have taken place to the iconography within the building in recent years. On the initiative of David Horsfield, the librarian, and with the enthusiastic support of students, images of political campaigns have been commemorated in the public displays in the library through badges, miners' banners and Wapping printers' memorabilia. Individual students have also been celebrated in the fabric of the building with institutional support. The first such initiative was in honour of David Kitson, the South African anti apartheid campaigner, who was both a student at the College in 1952 and, after his release from prison, a tutor in the 1980s. As part of the campaign to press for his release the most recent block in Walton Street was named in his honour in 1980. In less happy circumstances, in the 1990s trees, benches and plaques have been erected in memory of students who have died in tragic circumstances including Dennis Russell, a literature student, commemorated by a bench inscribed 'Bloody Middlemarch!' and Margaret Adams, murdered by her estranged husband while studying at Ruskin, and remembered through a plaque and cherry tree at the Headington site.

It is significant that students themselves have attached so much importance to such changes to the fabric of the buildings even though they spend very little of their lives at the place – two years for full time courses until 1993, since when the Certificate in Higher Education has been a one year course.[29] It is a measure of the impact that the College is perceived to have had upon their lives that students should feel the need to place their mark physically upon the place. Students still use the Bodleian library, attend university lectures and frequent the Oxford Union (they do so more for the cheap beer than the company) yet they are not part of the Oxford University. Nor are they part of a conventionally described working-class community. The very act of applying to and then attending Ruskin denotes an act of being set apart from their peers. As one student explained at the centenary, 'People who came from the shopfloor, from industry, found it very difficult to go back and to be part of that culture'.[30]

In the 1990s rupture and discontinuity have been the norm. Typically, application to the College may follow a lengthy period of unemployment brought on by the decline of industry, physical disability or 'blacklisting'. Others come after a difficult divorce, or domestic violence. But it is not the lack of work or domestic security per se which brings the student to Ruskin but the final realisation, often after a number of years, that their former life no longer exists and cannot be reclaimed. Material change has usually been accompanied by emotional upheaval: instability has been the characteristic of at least their recent lives. Unsurprisingly in these circumstances, students often desire to use their time at college to make more sense of the world and their place within it. How they see themselves and how they want to be seen become important in underpinning a sense of who they are.[31]

For many students, where they are studying and living – within the Walton Street or Headington buildings – is the self same place.

Indeed by coming to study most single students become de facto homeless and thus the physical surroundings become even more significant as both a temporary home and simultaneously the reason for a lack of permanent housing. As one tutor is accustomed to saying at prospective student interviews, 'It's a bit like living in a pressure cooker and a goldfish bowl'. Disputes about noise, late night drinking, and personality clashes become exacerbated when living in a confined space, and individual disagreements frequently become transformed into institutional preoccupations. This elision between personal and public space might explain the way that ex-student narratives about Ruskin have frequently included the College building almost as a protagonist. As Stan Brumby, a student at the College in 1931-3, recalled for the centenary celebrations:

> I have many memories of Ruskin ... when Gandhi visited Ruskin – we gathered in the Matron's room where Gandhi sat in the centre of the room ... One other memory I will mention is one Sunday afternoon in what was then the library. Some of the ladies made tea and toast in the Library. They were pleasant times.[32]

In the plethora of autobiographies of former Ruskin male students there have been common themes: prolific examples of students grappling with essay writing, attending tedious lectures and developing good study habits. But the domestic arrangements also loomed large, as Nick Kneale explores in his chapter in this book. The (former) obligation to carry out cleaning and washing up was apparently an unexpected task for working-class male students even though what was required was no different to the work routinely carried out in their own homes by their womenfolk.[33] That such incidents feature in a genre of writing devoted to an exploration of the self and, conventionally, a sense of developing and changing is itself significant. Ruskin College was not just seen as an educational institution affecting the intellect but one which influenced even the minutiae of everyday life.

INSTITUTIONAL CHANGES TO THE BUILDING

The mid-1990s were not a happy time for Ruskin nor the rest of the adult education sector. Beset by financial crises, inspections, internal restructurings and uncertainty, which affected both those who studied and were employed in the place, the mood was out of joint with the images presented within the College building of certainty and fixedness. Then in late 1996 Raphael Samuel, who had taught History at the College from 1963, died from cancer. To many both inside and outside the College he epitomised within their memory their sense of Ruskin College, as Paul Martin has discussed in his chapter in this collection. Only one member of staff, Johnny Cistone, the handyman, had had a longer service record: Raphael Samuel was perceived as 'always having been there'. In his very manner and style he had invited mythic tales. Indeed memorial events at the College and at the packed Conway Hall in London's Red Lion Square were peppered with witty anec-dotes and fond stories of eccentric – but loved – behaviour. In some ways he could have been seen as the very embodiment of a sense of continuity, which Ruskin College had tried so hard to construct institutionally. But in his years at Ruskin he had constantly disrupted such a narrative both with a rigorous intellectual chal-lenge to conformity and organisationally through the History Workshop Conferences and the pedagogic demands placed upon students.[34] As Alison Light, Raphael Samuel's partner and posthu-mous editor put it, 'It was Ruskin College's marginal and oppositional place in Oxford and in higher education that he savoured, and where he belonged for over thirty years'.[35] College staff discussed about how best the College might remember him.[36] One suggestion was to re-name Buxton hall in his memory. As archive photographs indicate, this had been the location of so many History Workshop conferences, the Malcolm X rally of 1970, and frequent public meetings supporting workers in struggle. Yet the place was still named after a former tutor who had epito-mised conformity and accommodation and who had preserved the ethos of the College in the wake of the student strike of 1909. Some staff did not want to disrupt the previous narratives – though many knew little of their content – perhaps fearing that this might signal further change and upheaval in a workplace characterised by uncertainty. Others suggested that a small place, such as a library room, would remind them more appropriately of Raphael Samuel with his carefully untidy small study.

But the historians on the staff who had first pressed for the changes were apparently convincing: in Summer 1997 the Raphael Samuel Hall was opened. The hall was re-hung with new images and the heavy portrait of Sanderson Furniss (he who had hardly ever spoken to a working man except gardeners, coachmen, and gamekeepers) displaced.[37] Instead there were displays of publications, *History Workshop Journal* and *New Left Review*, both of which Raphael Samuel had edited. A framed photograph of the sacked principal, Dennis Hird, was re-hung in this main hall; in due course a small painting of Raphael by Peter Donaldson was displayed and postcard reproductions sold as a centenary fund raising venture.[38] In time over the main entrance there would be a wooden plaque hand crafted and gilded by a former student. In death Raphael Samuel became remembered in the public spaces of the building in ways previously reserved for those operating within the very different sorts of intellectual traditions which he had challenged throughout his life.

It would, however, be erroneous to assume that institutionally the College had broken from previous traditions by the re-naming of Buxton Hall. At a similar time that college staff and former students were commemorating the influence of Raphael Samuel, the College management re-named and re-decorated another room, on the Headington site, in conventional ways. The Morris room was opened replete with hideous juxtaposed modern paintings of the socialist William Morris, Bill Morris, the Transport and General Workers Union secretary, and William Morris (Lord Nuffield) the anti-union and anti-semite founder of the Oxford car company. To this anachronistic counterposition were added a wall of photographs of grey men in suits redolent of the worst iconography of British trade unionism. In many ways these two rooms represent the tensions which coexist at Ruskin: a backward looking conservatism rooted in an idealised conformist labourist past; or a future which builds on contested understandings of the past and acknowledges different political and cultural debates and

Raphael Samuel by Peter Donaldson

identities outside the mainstream. As I write, plans are afoot to consolidate the College on one site and to rebuild it entirely. While clearly there are a plethora of planning and financial issues at stake, it is nevertheless fascinating to note that it is likely that the Jericho site with its particular geographical contradictions will remain. The present building has embodied much of the contestation of different forms of knowledge and experience within its fabric and iconography. Certainly most of the recent changes owe more to the students and staff working in the place than the earlier plans enacted in 1912. Ruskin College has been the focus of different and multiple attempts to create consensual – and oppositional – identities. Whatever form the new building takes it will assuredly still be such a contested place.

Thanks to past and present History students with whom I have discussed many of the ideas in this article. Particular thanks to Clifford Jones, and Bill Whitehead for sharing their own research. Also thanks to Katherine Hughes, Paul Martin and David Horsfield for their helpful comments.

NOTES

1. Harold Pollins, *The History of Ruskin College*, Ruskin College library, Oxford 1984, pp68-70.
2. Ruskin centenary gala brochure, Ruskin College, Oxford 1999, p44.
3. Comments by Alexandra Fraser and Natalie Stear from interviews conducted by Bill Whitehead, 20 February 1999. Tape in Ruskin College library.
4. Raphael Samuel, *Island Stories*, Verso, London 1998 p363. See too Doreen Massey, 'Places and their pasts', *History Workshop Journal*, 39, 1995, pp89-112; Doreen Massey, 'Space-time and the politics of location' in James Lingwood (ed), Rachel Whiteread, *House*, Phaidon, London 1995.
5. Currently the most recently available census returns. Census returns for Worcester Place, 1891, Family Records Centre, London.
6. Ruskin College, Oxford. Opening of new buildings and unveiling of the Buxton memorial, 22 February 1913: Report of the proceedings, as quoted in Pollins, *op.cit.*, p26.
7. John Ruskin, *The Stones of Venice*, Vol.1, new edition, George Allen, London 1898, p35.
8. Robert Hewison, 'John Ruskin and the argument of the age' in Susan Casteras, Susan Phelps Gordon et al, *John Ruskin and the Victorian Eye*, Harry N. Abrams, New York 1993, pp28-51.
9. See Hilda Kean, 'Myths of Ruskin College', *Studies in the Education of Adults*, vol. 28:2, October 1996, pp217-8.
10. Amne Grafflin divorced her husband Walter Vrooman in 1903 on grounds of infidelity. Walter was committed to a state hospital in New York in 1904 and died there in 1909, aged forty. Ross E. Paulson, *Radicalism and Reform. The Vrooman Family and American Social Thought 1837-1937*, University of Kentucky Press, Kentucky 1968, pp147-150, 183.

11. John Ruskin, *Time and Tide by Weare and Tyne. Twenty Five Letters to a Working Man of Sunderland*, fifth edition, Smith, Elder & Co., London 1894, p11.

12. John Ruskin, *The Stones of Venice*, Vol.3, appendix 7, as quoted in J.A.Hobson, *John Ruskin Social Reformer*, third edition, James Nisbet & Co., London 1904, p241. Such comments were directed specifically to the education of men. See John Ruskin, *Sesame and Lilies*, J.M. Dent, London 1907, for his views on female education.

13. Walter Vrooman's speech at the inaugural meeting of Ruskin Hall. Jackson's *Oxford Journal*, 25 February 1899, Ruskin College archive press cuttings file.

14. See Anne Phillips and Tim Putnam, 'Education for emancipation: the movement for independent working class education 1908-1928', *Capital and Class*, 10, 1980.

15. Raymond Williams, *Politics and Letters: Interviews with New Left Review*, New Left Books, London 1979, p79.

16. Sanderson Furniss, *Memories*, pp83-4, as quoted in J.P.M. Millar, *The Labour College Movement*, NCLC, London 1977, p9. Charles Buxton, the College vice principal and acting principal when the socialist principal Dennis Hird was sacked, referred to the work of the College as an 'idealist experiment in faeces Romuli'.

17. Pollins 1984, *op.cit.*, pp24-5.

18. Memorandum of Association of Ruskin Hall, Ruskin College archive.

19. Richard Hofstadter, *The Progressive Historians: Turner, Beard, Parrington*, Alfred A. Knopf, 1968, p345, as quoted in Michael Kraus and Davis D. Joyce, *The Writing of American History*, University of Oklahoma Press, Oklahoma, revised edition, 1985, p265.

20. It was Beard's suggestion that the institution be named after John Ruskin who he so admired. Paulson, *op.cit.*, pp147; Kraus and Joyce, *op.cit.*, pp252-265.

21. Probably more interesting than it might sound. Beard's Economic Interpretation of the American Constitution emphasised the holdings of the founding fathers of public securities, Hofstadter 1968, *op.cit.*,pp175, 207.

22. Judy Mabro, *I Ban Everything*, Ruskin College library, Oxford 1985.

23. Dave Renton, *Red Shirts and Black. Fascists and Anti-Fascists in Oxford in the 1930s*, Ruskin College library, Oxford 1996.

24. Sally Alexander, Interview, in Michelene Wandor, *Once a feminist. Stories of a generation*, Virago, London 1990; H.D. Hughes, 'Correspondence' in *History Workshop Journal*, 11, spring 1981.

25. Plans for a Women's Liberation Conference thirty years on are currently

being discussed through the Oxford Women's Research Network.

26. Hilda Kean 1996, *op.cit.*, p218.

27. The achievements of Miss Lister, a bright economics student and student rep after the 1914-8 war, were unknown. Yet at the time she was admired as the best student at Marxian economics. As fellow student George Hodgkinson wrote home: 'Marx's treatises on Capital in three volumes are terrible reading but I understand that Miss Lister has read them. She is a full blown Bolshie and advertises the fact though by wearing a blood red knitted sports coat.' Unpublished letters from George Hodgkinson to May Hodgkinson 17 October 1919, p11 and 26 November 1919, p53, Ruskin College archive.

28. Samuel, 1998, *op.cit.*, p367.

29. Although social work students and those taking postgraduate M.A. courses are students for a longer period, those taking the more traditional form of courses are here for shorter periods.

30. Annie Skinner, from interview conducted by Bill Whitehead, 20 February 1999. Tape in Ruskin College library.

31. See Hilda Kean, 'Continuity and change: the identity of the political reader', *Changing English*, vol.3:2, 1996, pp209-218; Hilda Kean, 'Radical Adult Education: the Reader and the Self' in Marjorie Mayo and Jane Thompson (eds), *Adult Learning, Critical Intelligence and Social Change*, NIACE 1995, pp58-68.

32. Stan Brumby, Ruskin's centenary gala brochure, *op.cit.*, p14.

33. Hilda Kean 1996, *op.cit.*, p214. See too 'A Woman hits back' in *Young Oxford*, 1:1, October 1899.

34. See, for example, debate in *History Workshop Journal* 11, spring 1981; Harold Pollins, 'History Workshop: the making of a myth', *Society for the Study of Labour History Bulletin*, No.42, spring 1982, pp16-18. See also *Raphael Samuel 1934-1996: Tributes and Appreciations*, privately published, 1997.

35. Alison Light, 'Note on text', Samuel 1998, *op.cit.*, pxxi.

36. There was also the proposal, still not fully implemented, that given that Raphael Samuel had died of lung cancer, the College should at last move into the contemporary world and ban smoking.

37. See note 16.

38. Bizarrely a photograph was also included of Raphael's study which some thought epitomised their idea of an academic's den (rather than what some might read as a carefully constructed Dickensian set piece).

Contributors

Geoff Andrews is a former Ruskin student. He is currently Senior Lecturer in Politics at the University of Hertfordshire, and an Associate Lecturer at the Open University. He has written for a range of newspapers and journals including *The Guardian, The New Statesman* and the *THES*. He recently co-edited *New Left, New Right and Beyond*, 1999.

Richard Bryant has been a tutor on the Ruskin Applied Social Studies courses since 1979 and has also worked as a community worker in Glasgow and Oxford. He has written extensively on the financial circumstances of adult students.

Roger Fieldhouse was a tutor organiser for the WEA in North Yorkshire before becoming a staff member of the Extra Mural Department at the University of Leeds. His main interests lie in the politics and history of adult education and he is the lead contributor and editor of a *History of Modern British Adult Education*. Since 1986 he has been Professor of Adult Education and Director of Continuing Education at the University of Exeter.

Hilda Kean is a tutor in History at Ruskin College. She is the course director of the MA in Popular Memory and Public History and convenes the Ruskin Public History discussion group. She has published widely in historical and cultural studies. Her most recent book is *Animal Rights. Political and Social Change in Britain since 1800* (1998). She is currently researching into local and family history in East London.

Nick Kneale is a tutor in English Studies and Creative Writing at Ruskin College. He has also taught at the universities of Warwick and Reading and at the Open University. His Cambridge Ph.D thesis examines representations of maleness in Victorian literature and he is a regular reviewer in the field of gender studies for *The Modern Language Review*.

Paul Martin is a tutor in history at Ruskin College. He is also Associate Lecturer in material culture at the Department of Museum Studies, University of Leicester. His interests are various but especially focus on visual and popular culture and public history. His latest book is *Popular Collecting And The Everyday Self: The Reinvention of Museums?*, Leicester University Press, 1999. He is currently working on a projected book on the cultures of consumption and community in popular music.

Bob Purdie was a Ruskin student 1974-6. He subsequently studied in the Universities of Warwick and Strathclyde. He returned to Ruskin as Tutor in Politics in 1988. He is the author of *Politics in the Streets*, Blackstaff, Belfast 1990.

Jane Thompson teaches Women's Studies at Ruskin College and is a Research Associate at the University of Warwick. She is currently seconded to the National Institute of Adult Continuing Education to do work on educational responses to the 'social exclusion' and 'widening participation' agendas. Her publications include *Adult Education for a Change* (1980), *Learning Liberation: Women's Response to Men's Education* (1983), *Learning the Hard Way: Women's Oppression in Men's Education* (1989), *Adult Learning, Critical Intelligence and Social Change* (edited with M. Mayo 1995), *Words in Edgeways: Radical Learning for Social Change* (1997), *Out From Under: Women, Class and Education* (2000).